Once you've enjoyed this book, you can now listen to H. N. Lloyd discussing true crime cases on the Murder Tales Podcast. It's available to listen to for free on Apple Podcasts, Anchor, Spotify or wherever you listen to your favourite podcasts.

Building a relationship with my readers is very important to me. I occasionally send newsletters with details on new releases, special offers, podcast news and the exclusive freebies just for my fans, such as exclusive Murder Tales Shorts and Freekly Oldacre novellas only available to subscribers. You can get access to all this exciting stuff by signing up for the newsletter here https://mailchi.mp/bf0d6fb45630/hnlloydnewsletter. And don't forget to like the Murder Tales Facebook page https://www.facebook.com/crimediscussion/.

Murder Tales:

Murdered Because She Was A Woman

A True Crime Anthology

By

H. N. Lloyd

Content

Introduction

This book came about after a conversation between myself and Chris 'Kristof' Britton, the producer and co-host of the Murder Tales Podcast. We were recording an episode about a case that features in this collection. The murder of Diane Sindall was a huge local event when we were both children. The investigation seemed to drag on for weeks, and the fear it caused in the local community was palpable. During a break in recording, we discussed the cases we remembered from childhood. Many of them are now long forgotten by the wider public. As a rather morbid child, I vividly remember the monthly excitement of being allowed to stay up late and watch my favourite TV show, Crimewatch UK. Many of the reconstructions of the murders were etched upon my mind due to the frisson of fear they instilled in me.

Kristof suggested that I research some of the cases I remembered from those Crimewatch UK reconstructions and write a book about them. I thought it was a good idea and duly got down to earmarking out some of the cases that had haunted my mind since childhood, thanks to that wonderful show. As I wrote, I realised that a theme was naturally arising from the cases I had picked— sexually motivated murders. When I realised this, I decided to widen the net and include cases that hadn't featured on what had once been my favourite childhood television show.

Therefore, the twelve cases in this collection are a mixed bag of classic true crime cases, some of them solved, some of them infuriating enduring mysteries. They encompass a sixty-year period from the 1950s to the 2010s and take place both in the United Kingdom and the United States. The title of the book '*Murdered Because She Was A Woman*' comes from the memorial of that very murder victim we were discussing on the day of the book's genesis. This phrase literally applies to all of the victims in this book. They were murdered for no other reason other than the fact they were women. This book is dedicated to their memories. It is a book about those victims as much as it is about the mindset and psychology of the killers themselves.

I hope these dozen cases enrapture and chill you as much as many of them did me when I was a child.

H. N. Lloyd

The Teddington Towpath Murders: Barbara Songhurst and Christine Reed

The Teddington Towpath Murders shocked the nation at a time of national celebration. As the country basked in a heatwave and looked forward to the coronation of Queen Elizabeth II, the sexually motivated murder of two young girls seized the headlines. It's a sickening tale that still packs a punch to this day.

Christine Reed was eighteen, and her friend Barbara Songhurst was just sixteen. Christine was born on Monday the 18th of March 1935, to Herbert and Lucy Reed, the middle of three children. Barbara was born on Thursday the 29th of April 1937, the fifth of ten children born to Daniel and Gertrude Songhurst. They had both attended Victoria Girls School where, despite the two-year age difference, the two girls soon became best of friends. Barbara easily excelled in her exams, but Christine struggled. Whilst she ultimately scraped through her examinations, Christine was described as being "educationally challenged" by her teachers. Nevertheless, with their education behind them, both girls had set about finding work of their own so that they could support their families.

Barbara's father, Daniel Songhurst, was unable to work due to an industrial accident where he had broken his back. So, Barbara helped the family finances by working as a dispenser for Harwood and Halls Chemists, earning £1 15 shillings a week (roughly £60 a week when accounting for inflation). Over half of Barbara's wages were given over to her mother to help the family. In her spare time, Barbara was a local beauty queen who regularly attended local beauty pageants. Herbert Reed earned a minimum wage as a shopworker, and Lucy Reed was profoundly deaf. In a world that made no accommodations for this disability, she found it impossible to find work. So, Christine obtained employment in a local factory where she earned £3 18 shillings a week (roughly £150 when accounting for inflation). Just like Barbara, Christine gave over half her wages to her mother to help with the family finances.

Despite being the elder of the two girls, Christine was described as being the shyer, less chatty and more retiring of the two friends. The police would later describe both girls as "*virtuous.*" This, in all probability, was veiled 1950s language for both girls having been virgins. The two teenage girls both lived in Teddington, a district of the now affluent London borough of Richmond-Upon-Thames. However, the girls did not come from well-off families. Indeed, even at the age of sixteen, Barbara was still having to share a bed with her younger sister.

Both girls loved nothing better than a good bicycle ride. One of the nicest places for them to cycle during that barmy summer was along the banks of the River Thames. On Sunday the 31st of May 1953, Christine and Barbara did just this. After attending church, they met up at the nearby Blue Angel Café, and then they cycled up and down a four-mile stretch of the idyllic towpath several times, returning to Teddington Lock on more than one occasion to talk to some boys who were camping out on Ham Fields. The three 'boys' were called John Alan Wells, Albert Sparkes and Peter Warren. John Alan Wells was a twenty-one-year-old architectural student, and he knew Christine well.

They had been friends for five years and five weeks before Christine had introduced John to Barbara. A little romance was budding between John and Barbara, and when they thought no one was looking, the young couple would steal a kiss together. Christine and Barbara's last visit to the campsite where John and his friends camped was at 8.00 p.m. On this occasion, the two girls had sat chatting with the boys until 11.00 p.m. when they told the lads they intended to cycle home.

The last sighting of Christine and Barbara was half an hour later when two campers by the name of Basil Nixon and Sheila Danes saw the girls cycling along a little further up the towpath. A few minutes later, Basil and Sheila both heard several screams.

When the two girls didn't return home that night, their parents contacted the police. It was a sleepless night that turned into a mournful morning. A foreman for the Port of London Authority named George Costa found Barbara's body dumped into the Thames, two miles downstream from the last sighting. There were three deep stab wounds in her back, penetrating into both her lungs and her heart. She had vicious head injuries; her skull was fractured, and her cheekbone was completely crushed. Her back and legs were covered in bruises, grazes and lacerations. As a final indignity, the killer had taken her virginity in an act of bestial rape. After carrying out the autopsy, pathologist Dr Keith Mount said that the attack had been carried out by "*an expert rapist.*"

At first, the investigation into the murder of Barbara Songhurst and the disappearance of Christine Reed was decidedly lacklustre. The investigation was understaffed as most of the Metropolitan Police Force were involved in preparations for the coronation. London was experiencing record numbers of visitors, and most police officers were being used for crowd control. Chief Superintendents Rudkin and Hannam were placed in charge of the investigation, and a handful of uniformed officers were assigned to the case. They set about carrying out a search of the area around the towpath. They discovered Christine and Barbara's shoes and socks close to a patch of bloodstained daisies. From here, a trail of blood led from this most likely scene of the murder to the spot on the towpath where Barbara's body had been discarded into the river.

Police dragged a section of the River Thames using electromagnets. One of the first things that the electromagnetic plucked from the murky depths of the river was Christine's distinctive silver and blue coloured sports bicycle. The bicycle was just 100 yards from the site where Barbara Songhurst had most likely been murdered. Later, police had the river dried out for a three-mile stretch between Teddington and the Richmond Half-Lock so that they could search for further evidence and hopefully find the murder weapon. Unfortunately, this clever endeavour proved fruitless.

The police were under strict orders not to upset the coronation tourists and ruin what should have been such a special day for them. And so, as police combed the streets and carried out house-to-house enquiries, frogmen searched the river, and the locks were closed, and sections of the river dried up, a public address system was set up, which reassuringly relayed the message to the gathered public that the police were definitely not looking for dead bodies. They were simply there to ensure the safety of the crowds.

On Saturday the 6th of June 1953, Christine Reed's body was finally found by a group of tourists. Christine's body had floated into a clump of weeds by Glover's Island, a mile downstream from Richmond Bridge. Like Barbara, Christine's skull was fractured. She had six deep stab wounds to her chest. Christine had also been raped, not just once, but ten times. The attack upon Christine had seemingly been more frenzied and brutal than the one carried out upon Barbara. In a heartbreaking twist, Christine had survived the brutal and sustained attack and had ultimately drowned when her assailant tossed her body into the water like so much trash. Dr Mount was sickened by the injuries inflicted. After completing the autopsy, he told the police, *"This is the work of a maniac. This murderer is a monster as strong as an ape."*

Initially, the police believed that two men were involved in the murders, one holding Christine whilst Barbara was attacked, raped and murdered. Then Duncan Webb got involved in the investigation. Webb was the crime reporter for the top-selling newspaper of the day, The News of the World, in a time long before that particular publication fell into disrepute, scandal and ignominious closure. Webb took an interest in the case as he had been in the area of the murder on the night in question. He came forward when any men who had been in the Teddington district on the night of the attacks were asked to come forward and eliminate themselves from enquiries. Webb also had a good working relationship with the police. He took the opportunity to have a quiet chat with Superintendent Rudkin about the case. Rudkin told Webb that in his thirty years as a police officer, he had never seen such horrific injuries inflicted upon a murder victim. As they chatted about the case, Webb postulated two things: (a) the same person committed both murders, and (b) the killer had possibly thrown the murder weapon at one of the victims to incapacitate them whilst he had his wicked way with the other.

Now, this might have sounded a little far-fetched. After all, this was Teddington and not the Wild West, but Superintendent Rudkin felt that Webb was onto something. Had Barbara been running away from her killer, so the crazed killer had thrown the murder weapon which had impaled itself into Barbara's back? Superintendent Rudkin gave this theory serious consideration, and he had several travelling circus and variety knife-throwing acts brought in and questioned. Superintendent Hannam wasn't completely happy with this line of enquiry. He felt it was a waste of the investigation's limited resources. He didn't think that the killer was some itinerant knife-throwing nutter. He believed the killer was most likely a local man.

Superintendent Hannam was experienced and tenacious. Known affectionately to his men as 'The Count' due to his upper-middle-class roots and posh accent, it was once said that his solid and no-nonsense approach to policing made him "*the policeman's policeman.*" Hannam ensured that as many of the local populace were interviewed as possible, especially the adult males. Statements and the alibis of 1600 local men were taken and checked. Questionnaires were distributed to all local residents. Police paid visits to all the local hotels, guesthouses and bed and breakfasts and asked for the names and contact details of all the guests who had been staying on the night of the murder. The guests were all tracked down, interviewed and had their alibis verified. 900 American Air Force men from nearby Camp Griffiss were spoken to, their kits were examined, and their alibis verified. Uniformed officers were sent to local pubs, cafes, churches, and dance halls, where they announced their presence and asked for anyone with any information, no matter how insignificant it might seem, to come forward and make themselves known. Every avenue of investigation drew a blank.

On Thursday the 18th of June 1953, Police Constable Arthur Cosh had been detailed with cleaning the police cars at Kingston-Upon-Thames Police Station. Under the front seat of one of the police cars, he found an axe. Rather than reporting the find to his superiors, PC Cosh put the axe in his locker but then fell ill whilst on duty and was off sick for the next five days. When he returned to duty, he found that no one had enquired about the axe, so he took it home and began to use it to cut up kindling wood. PC Cosh gave absolutely no thought to how significant this axe could be to the ongoing double murder investigation.

The real break in the case came by luck rather than clever policing. On Sunday the 28th of June 1953, a suspicious-looking man was spotted hitchhiking on Sandy Lane in Esher, Surrey (some six miles from Teddington). A passing motorist slowed down and was taken by how much the hitchhiker fitted the description of a man wanted for raping a fourteen-year-old girl in the village of Oxshott, Surrey. A month before, on Sunday the 24th of May 1953, Kathleen Ringham had been walking her dog on Oxshott Heath. A young man had snuck up behind her and bashed her over the head with the handle of an axe. He then dragged her into some nearby bushes and raped her. Despite being deeply traumatised, Kathleen was able to give the police an excellent description of her assailant, which subsequently received widespread publicity. He was a man in his early twenties, strong-looking, with brown hair, a spotty complexion and a cleft chin.

The public-minded motorist drove to the nearest police station and told the desk sergeant that he believed the Oxshott rapist was hitchhiking just around the corner. Police Constables Oliver and Howard raced around to the spot where the man was trying to thumb a lift and managed to detain him before he had a chance to secure a ride.

Before the evening was out, the hitchhiker had been positively identified by Kathleen Ringham and a lady named Patricia Birch, whom the hitchhiker had attempted to rape on Friday the 12th of June 1953, in Windsor Park. The hitchhiker found himself being charged with rape and attempted rape.

The rapist hitchhiker was a twenty-two-year-old unemployed labourer and petty thief by the name of Alfred Charles Whiteway. He was from Teddington. The fourth of eight children born to Alfred Senior and Mary Jane Elizabeth Whiteway. He was a happily married[i] father with one infant child and another child on the way. Whiteway's mother-in-law couldn't abide him and had banned him from her home. This left the young married couple forced to catch intimate moments alone in the alleyway at the back of his wife's parents' house. He lived in a tiny council flat with his mother and siblings, sleeping on the kitchen floor with his Uncle Charlie.

Intriguingly, Whiteway had a collection of knives, including a large Gurkha knife. Indeed, Whiteway was an adept self-taught knife-thrower. One of his party tricks was throwing an axe forty yards into a chalk line drawn onto a piece of wood. As the police learned more about Whiteway, they became utterly intrigued, especially when they learned that Whiteway had a connection to one of the Teddington Towpath murder victims. Whiteway was good friends with Barbara Songhurst's brother, Daniel, and he had once been engaged to Daniel's sister-in-law, Josephine Knight.

Whiteway had no convictions for violence, although he was known to the police. Whiteway's criminal behaviours began when he was eleven, as his father was fighting a long, painful and ultimately fatal battle with cancer. His antecedents were all for larceny; he had spent time in prison for theft, and in his youth, his criminal behaviours had led to him spending some time at the Cotswold Approved School, a borstal for boys with emotional and behavioural problems. This disruption to his education had left Whiteway illiterate. The headmaster of the approved school noted that Whiteway had a predilection for being *"foul-mouthed and cruel to animals."* It was also said that he was bully towards the other boys and *"sexually aggressive"* towards the female staff members.

After being released from the approved school, Whiteway had wanted to join the army, but he failed the medical due to poor eyesight, and the assessors also had serious concerns about his intelligence. This rejection from the armed services was said to have severely shaken Whiteway's confidence, and for a long period afterwards, he seemed directionless and lacked motivation in his life. For the next three years, he drifted from one temporary job to the next. Never holding down any one job for longer than a couple of months.

Despite the claims of bullying, sexual aggression and cruelty, Ellen Whiteway and several of his ex-girlfriends all said Alfred Charles Whiteway was a perfect gentleman. There was no hint of domestic violence or kinky proclivities in his relationships or sexual behaviours. However, the exact circumstances of how he met his wife were distinctly odd. Whiteway was twenty years old. He stalked sixteen-year-old Ellen Jones and her friend from a playground where they had been hanging out, and followed her over a mile to her home, where he loitered outside her parent's house for several hours. When Ellen re-emerged on an errand, Whiteway finally approached her and struck up a conversation. They dated for only four months before Whiteway asked Ellen to marry him. Ellen's parents deeply disapproved of the relationship. They not only thought Whiteway was far too old for their daughter, but they also found him to be immature, coarse, creepy and uncivilised, and they forbade the marriage. To force their hand, Whiteway impregnated Ellen, leading to a shotgun wedding that neither family was happy with. The hastily convened nuptials took place on Wednesday the 27th of February 1952, and their daughter, Christine, was born a few short months later on Tuesday the 20th of May 1952. Whiteway missed the birth of his daughter as he was serving yet another prison sentence for burglary.

Whiteway had been interviewed as part of the Tedding Towpath enquiries, but his wife, Ellen, and Uncle Charlie had given him an alibi for the night of the murder. He'd been visiting Ellen at her parent's house in Kingston-Upon-Thames. He hadn't left until nearly midnight, far too late for him to have been the murderer.

The police asked Whiteway where the axe was that he used in his axe-throwing party trick. Whiteway told the police it was stored in a cupboard in his mother's house in Sydney Road, Teddington. The house was searched, but the axe couldn't be found. Whiteway was asked again. This time, Whiteway made an absolutely astonishing admission. Some weeks before, he had been picked up for questioning in Weybridge about the attempted rape of Patricia Birch. At the time of his detention, he had been armed with the axe, and so he had hidden it under the passenger seat of the police car. On that occasion, he had been able to give a suitable account of himself, and he had been released from police custody with an apology.

Superintendent Hannam raced to Kingston-Upon-Thames Police Station and asked what had become of the axe found under the passenger seat of one of their police cars. At first, Hannam was met by a parade of blank and confused faces until, sheepishly, Police Constable Cosh admitted that he had taken it home and used it to break up firewood. He went home and returned with the axe, and to Superintendent Hannam's fury, he discovered that any valuable forensic evidence had been obliterated. It was covered in PC Cosh's fingerprints. The blade had been blunted by overuse, and it was covered in sawdust. The axe was evidentially useless, and due to the break in the chain of custody, it would be inadmissible at any future trial. However, all was not lost. The pathologist was able to confirm that the axe was probably the murder weapon, as it was capable of making identical wounds to those found on the victim's bodies. Better luck was had when Whiteway's clothes were forensically examined. Microscopic traces of blood were discovered on his shoes and shoelaces.

What happened next has been disputed. The official version has it that Superintendents Hannam and Rudkin confronted Whiteway with the axe and the information about the blood being found on his shoes. Whiteway was said to have immediately cracked, saying, *"You know bloody well it was me. It's all up, you know bloody well I done it… What a bloody mess. I'm mental. I must have a fucking woman. I can't stop myself… Put that chopper away. It haunts you… I can't stop myself."* Whiteway then gave a detailed confession to the two murders. Whiteway disputed this. He claimed that he had never confessed and had been tricked into signing a blank piece of paper onto which the police later wrote a false confession. He would continue these denials at trial. However, Whiteway irrevocably damaged this defence when he verbally repeated the confession during a committal hearing at Richmond Magistrates Court on Tuesday the 15th of September 1953.

Alfred Charles Whiteway's trial commenced at the Old Bailey on Friday the 18th of September 1953, before Mr Justice Hilbery. Hilbery was a very well-respected judge who wrote '*Duty And Art In Advocacy,*' which for many years was a standard text that was given to any barrister who was called to the bar. The famed Senior Treasury Counsellor Christmas Humphries undertook the prosecution. Humphries was the lead prosecuting counsel in several famed miscarriages of justice and controversial prosecutions. He prosecuted Timothy Evans for the murder of his wife and daughter. Evans claimed his neighbour John Reginald Halliday Christie was the murderer. No one believed Evans at the time. However, it later transpired that Christie was one of post-war Britain's most prolific serial killers. He prosecuted poor old Derek Bentley for the murder of PC Sidney Miles. Bentley was a man with severe learning difficulties and an IQ that would have marked him out as having the emotional intelligence of a child. Bentley was found guilty of murder despite the fact he was in police custody for burglary at the time, and several police officers had witnessed the actual murderer, Michael Craig, pull the trigger. Humphries also prosecuted the last woman to be hanged for murder in England, Ruth Ellis. Ellis was suffering from severe trauma at the time of the murder due to the sustained campaign of domestic abuse she had suffered at the hands of the man she killed. Ellis had been persuaded to kill her abusive lover, David Blakely, by a bitter former lover called Desmond Cussen. Cussen had given Ellis the gun and taught Ellis how to use it. He had even driven her to the scene of the murder. Yet Cussen faced no prosecution for his central role in the crime[ii].

Whiteway was defended by an up-and-coming barrister by the name of Peter Rawlinson. Rawlinson was a war hero, having been mentioned in dispatches during World War II and having been seriously wounded in North Africa. An early advocate of LGBTQ[+] rights, he unsuccessfully defended author Peter Wildblood, one of the first people bold enough to publicly declare their homosexuality, when the author was prosecuted for gross indecency. Rawlinson would go on to become a Conservative MP, where he was appointed to the post of Solicitor General. When Prime Minister Margaret Thatcher thwarted Rawlinson's ambitions of becoming Lord Chief Justice, Rawlinson left politics and took up the directorship of the company that publishes the right-wing Daily Telegraph newspaper.

Despite the prosecution having what appeared to be a robust case against Whiteway, Rawlinson did the best he could to extricate his client from the hangman's noose. He kept Superintendent Hannam in the witness box for two whole days. He made Hannam look like a liar. He poked holes in Whiteway's confession that made it look entirely fabricated. He asked Hannam what he had meant when he once said that the law should sometimes be ignored to secure a conviction. Did this mean fitting people up? He left Hannam frustrated and bad-tempered. Despite these aspersions and allegations of corruption, Hannam was able to show that the confession couldn't have been fabricated in the way Whiteway claimed, as Whiteway had initialled over a dozen alterations and amendments to the confession as they had gone along.

Despite these valiant efforts on the part of Rawlinson, no one truly believed that Whiteway was innocent. The jury felt that even if the police had forged a confession, the young man was clearly guilty of the despicable crimes. On Saturday the 7th of November 1953, the jury retired to consider their verdict. It took them just forty-five minutes to return with a unanimous guilty verdict. The black cap was lowered onto Mr Justice Hilbery's head, and the sentence of death was pronounced.

Whiteway continued to protest his innocence, and an appeal was lodged on his behalf. On Monday the 7th of December 1953, the Lord Chief Justice Lord Goddard, Mr Justice Sellers and Mr Justice Barry re-examined the evidence. They concluded that the conviction was sound, and they gave permission for the execution to go ahead. Alfred Charles Whiteway was executed at Wandsworth Prison on Tuesday the 22nd of December 1953, by the famed hangman Albert Pierrepoint. Approximately 200 hundred people gathered outside the prison to watch the notice of execution be pinned to the prison door.

The capture and conviction of Alfred Charles Whiteway was said to be one of Scotland Yard's most notable successes in a century. Yet, as we have seen, Whiteway's capture was more due to luck rather than any great work of detective prowess. Indeed, the case was hampered by police bungling and ineptitude, which could have ruined any hope of a conviction. Yet, there can be little doubt that the right man was ultimately hanged for the crime. As much as I loathe capital punishment, I can't help feeling that for a man as bestial and depraved as Alfred Charles Whiteway, the punishment truly did fit the crime.

The Motorway Monster: Jacqueline Ansell-Lamb and Barbara Mayo

Jacqueline Susan Ansell-Lamb was born on Friday the 21st of September 1951, to Peter Ansell-Lamb and Jean Ansell-Lamb nee Fuller. Initially, it was a happy childhood growing up in and around the bustling streets of St Pancras and Islington in London. The family wanted for nothing. Peter Ansell-Lamb was a successful accountant, and his success afforded the family a comfortable middle-class lifestyle. The only blite came when Peter and Jean divorced in the late 1950s. Peter remarried in April 1962 and moved to Wembley, where he lived in White Castle Mansions. To Jacqueline, this felt like a rejection from the person she loved most in the world. Indeed, the divorce affected Jacqueline greatly. She lost interest in her studies and fell into a great depression. Peter Ansell-Lamb would later say, *"Jacci lost interest in everything. We had to take her to a psychiatrist. Once, we were contacted by the Samaritans after she had contemplated suicide."*

As Jacqueline entered puberty, she began to show signs of an unstable and spiteful personality. She could, at times, be completely unpredictable in her attitude and behaviour towards friends and family. Peter Ansell-Lamb explained, *"She could be a saint at times but could also be very cruel, even to people she loved. But no matter what Jacci did, I continued to love her."*

By the time the summer of love came about, Jacqueline might have been too young to partake of all its hedonism fully, but she fell in love with the ideals and spirit of the hippy counterculture. In a manner of speaking, it was another way for her to rebel and annoy her straight-laced parents. Jacqueline became *"very much a sixties teenager."* This hippy lifestyle caused conflict between Jacqueline and her parents. Jacqueline's mother attempted to try and get Jacqueline away from what she perceived as unhealthy influences and decided to move away from swinging London to the much more rural St Ives in Cambridgeshire. Jacqueline agreed it was time for a fresh start, but not in rural Cambridgeshire. Jacqueline's best friend, Judi Langrish, had recently moved to Manchester in the Northwest of England, and Jacqueline decided to follow her there.

By 1970, Jacqueline was living in a sprawling Victorian townhouse in Whalley Range, Manchester, where Jacqueline and Judi eked out an existence in a tiny attic flat that they rented for £4.50 a week (approximately £70 today when equating for inflation) from a lady called Katherine Hall. Ms Hall described Jacqueline as *"a beautiful girl, refined, and well-mannered."* To pay the rent, Jacqueline got a job as a legal secretary.

When Jacqueline got time off, she would often return to London and visit friends. This is precisely what Jacqueline and Judi Langrish did on the weekend that spanned Friday the 6th to Sunday the 8th of March 1970. Judi bought a return train ticket for the trip, but to save money, Jacqueline decided to take the train to London and intended to hitchhike her way back home.

Jacqueline visited the house she had briefly shared with some friends and collected the last of her belongings. Jacqueline then got changed, ready to attend a party in the Earl's Court region of the city. Jacqueline beautified herself, put on a blonde wig and long fake eyelashes, and as an accessory, she carried a distinctive bag from Japanese Airlines where the company's logo incorporated her initials 'JAL.' At the party, Jacqueline hooked up with a twenty-three-year-old man called David Sykes. After the party, Jacqueline went with Sykes to his flat in Blackheath Park, where she spent the night. The following day, Jacqueline decided to spend the remainder of the weekend with Sykes. This decision appears to have caused some animosity between Jacqueline and Judi, and Judi returned to Manchester.

On Sunday the 8th of March 1970, David Sykes offered to drive Jacqueline to the M1, where she could start the arduous journey back to Manchester. At 2.30 p.m., Sykes dropped off Jacqueline in Hendon at the slip road leading to the M1. Sykes told Jacqueline that he was eager to meet her again on her next visit to London, and so she gave him her number. Jacqueline then hitched a ride with a fellow hitchhiker fifty miles to Buckinghamshire.

We don't know how Jacqueline travelled further up the country, but we do know she made it safe and well to Warrington in Cheshire. At approximately 9.00 p.m., Jacqueline entered the Poplar Transport Café at High Leigh just off junction 20 of the M6 motorway. Jacqueline may have arranged to meet someone in this transport café. One of the cooks, Delia Brown, witnessed a man come into the café and make a beeline straight for Jacqueline. The pair exchanged brief words before the man came to the counter and ordered two coffees. He then returned to Jacqueline's table with the two cups of coffee, and they sat talking for quite some considerable time.

Around 10.00 p.m., Jacqueline and the man left the Poplar Transport Café together, and they both got into the man's car and drove off. The car was certainly white in colour, and whilst it appeared to be a Jaguar, Mrs Brown couldn't be entirely certain about its make. The man was described as in his twenties, five foot nine inches tall, medium build with dark hair and dressed in a charcoal grey business suit, white shirt, dark tie and black shoes. Mrs Brown got the impression that he may have been a travelling salesman of some kind. His attire stood out, with it being a Sunday and the Poplar Transport Café not being the sort of establishment where the punters usually wore a suit and tie.

There was a later unconfirmed sighting of Jacqueline. This was close to midnight, two miles from the Poplar Transport Café on the A556 Manchester to Chester Road. A young couple returning home from a night out believed they drove past Jacqueline standing at the side of the road, sticking her thumb out for a lift. The couple vividly remembered commenting that they felt sorry for the poor girl as it had started to snow.

On Monday the 9th of March 1979, Jacqueline was reported missing after she failed to attend work, and it was established that her friends and family had no idea of her whereabouts.

It was five days later that Jacqueline's body was discovered by a ten-year-old boy who was out for a walk with his father, a local farmer named Ted Whittaker of Knowles Pit Farm. Jacqueline was found in a wooded area known as Square Wood just outside the village of Mere. This spot was just three miles from the Poplar Transport Café and a mile from the unconfirmed sighting on the A556. Jacqueline's skirt had been removed but was neatly folded and placed next to her body. Her patent leather shoes had also been removed by her killer and placed neatly on top of the skirt. She had been beaten, receiving excessive blows to the back of her head, and she had been strangled with an electric flex. She had also been raped. Her body had then been posed so that she was lying face down on the ground and had been covered with her long purple coat. The killer had taken a memento from the scene, two silver buttons removed from Jacqueline's coat.

The police began their murder investigation in earnest. It quickly became one of the largest murder hunts that the Cheshire Constabulary had seen, with over 120 officers involved in the investigation.

The police very quickly established the identity of the victim. David Sykes was tracked down and eliminated from the enquiry. One of the leads the police were most hopeful about was Jacqueline's 'little black book.' In this, Jacqueline had the names of all the men she slept with, and she had graded them on a A$^+$ to C- scale. Despite the police pinning their hopes on one of these men being the killer, all were traced, and all had cast-iron alibis. The police tried to track down the owner of the white Jaguar car seen at the Poplar Transport Café. This avenue of investigation hit a dead end.

Friends and family of Jacqueline were interviewed to see if they could think of any reason why someone would want to murder Jacqueline. It was Judie Langrish who gave the police a possible motive, *"With someone she liked and was attracted to; she could be very charming and pleasant. If a man made approaches and Jacqueline didn't find him attractive, she could be extremely blunt and even cruel. She would simply tell them where to go. I think this may have happened with the man who killed her. He probably lost his temper."*

Forensic analysis of Jacqueline's body uncovered microscopic carpet fibres that came from a carpet roll or sample. Coinciding with the last weekend that

Jacqueline spent in London, there had been a carpet exhibition at Earl's Court. Could the killer have been a rep for a carpet company? Did that explain the man in the smart business suit in the Poplar Transport Café? Could Jacqueline have met the murderous rep in Earl's Court? Police investigated this lead as far as they could, but it led nowhere.

As the investigation into Jacqueline Ansell-Lamb cooled, the killer struck again. Barbara Janet Mayo was born on Wednesday the 20th of March 1946, the daughter of Herbert Theodore Mayo and Marjorie Edna Mayo nee Patience. Barbara appears to have been a surprise late addition to the family. There was a seven-year gap between the birth of Barbara and her older brother. Indeed, Theodore was quite old to become a father again, he was fifty-five when Barbara was born, and Marjorie was forty. Nevertheless, Theodore and Marjorie were overjoyed to have a daughter, for tragically, their first daughter, Margaret, had died in 1935, aged just two.

Barbara grew up in Taplow, Bedfordshire. It was a happy childhood if her parents were a bit strict in that time when there was still a hangover from puritanical Victorian upbringings. The Mayo's were a prosperous family, definitely in the middle-class bracket, and money was something they didn't really have to worry about. Theodore was an academic, a well-respected geologist. However, in August 1965, Barbara suffered the first real tragedy in her life when Theodore Mayo died.

By 1970, Barbara was a twenty-four-year-old English graduate and was training to be a teacher. Barbara also had a side hustle trading cars. Barbara was quite successful at this side hustle and had £6143 in the bank, which would equate to approximately £90,000 today when equating for inflation.

On Monday the 12th of October 1970, Barbara had arranged to collect the car of David Pollard, her boyfriend, from a garage in Catterick, North Yorkshire. The car had broken down on a recent trip to County Durham, and they had been forced to abandon it temporarily in Yorkshire. With no car, Barbara decided to hitchhike. Barbara felt entirely comfortable hitchhiking. She'd hitchhiked all across Europe during a gap year. At 8.00 a.m. Barbara left the flat she shared with David Pollard at 40 Rockley Road in Hammersmith and caught the Tube to Hendon. Barbara began hitchhiking from the exact same spot that Jacqueline Ansell-Lamb had seven months before.

When Barbara didn't return home by lunchtime on Tuesday the 13th of October 1970, David telephoned the garage in Catterick, who confirmed that Barbara had not arrived to collect the car. Barbara was immediately reported missing. However, David was not happy with the police's immediate response to the missing person's enquiry, so he hired a private detective to try and find Barbara.

On Sunday the 18th of October 1970, a couple on honeymoon out for a stroll in the countryside discovered Barbara's body in a woodland glade near the village of Ault Hucknall in Derbyshire. The spot was close to Junction 29 of the M1. Barbara's murder was chillingly similar to Jacqueline Ansell-Lambs. Barbara had been beaten and received injuries to the back of her head. She had been strangled with a ligature and had been raped. Her body had then been positioned face down on the ground with her coat covering her body. Just like in Jacqueline's case, the killer had even taken a memento from the scene, this time taking with him Barbara's handbag.

Detective Chief Superintendent Charlie Palmer from the famed Scotland Yard Murder Squad was put in charge of the murder enquiry. He started with an exceedingly bold move. He had roadblocks put up at every junction along the entire 150-mile length of the M1, and he had every driver questioned. This led to the motorway becoming gridlocked and caused traffic pandemonium.

House-to-house enquiries in the local area drew reports of several residents seeing a white or cream-coloured car parked in the lane that led to the wood late on the evening of Monday the 12th of October. This vehicle wasn't a Jaguar but a Vauxhall Viva estate.

When the roadblocks drew no results, DCS Palmer gathered the press to watch a reconstruction of Barbara's last known movements. A WPC was dressed in the actual clothes that Barbara had been wearing on the day of the murder, and she was filmed leaving 40 Rockley Road and walking towards Shepherd's Bush Tube Station. It was hoped that this reconstruction would jog the memories of witnesses who hadn't realised that they had seen something significant. After the reconstruction, a member of the press asked DCS Palmer what his views were on women hitchhiking on the M1; he replied simply, "*Don't.*"

The reconstruction led to over 700 members of the public coming forward with potential leads. One of these leads came from a lorry driver from Kimberley, Nottinghamshire. He stated that he was driving a colleague home from work at approximately 4.00 p.m. on Monday the 12th of October, when he drove past "*a* nice-looking girl, *thumbing a lift*." The witness came to believe that he had seen Barbara. The witness remembered commenting to his passenger, "*If I hadn't got you with me, I'd give her a lift*." The witness then observed in his rearview mirror a light-coloured Morris Traveller stopping and picking the girl up. The Morris Traveller then followed the witness's vehicle onto the M1. The witness was able to see the driver of the Morris Traveller in his rearview mirror clearly and described him as being *"between 30 and 35 years old, of medium build with mousy hair brushed forward."* This witness's statement was supported by a second witness who said that they had served Barbara in a butcher's shop in Kimberley. The butcher stated that they had sold Barbara some faggots.

The police were so convinced by the Kimberley sightings that they had a photofit of the driver of the Morris Traveller created. They then tracked down the driver of every Morris Traveller on the roads of the United Kingdom. This was no small task. There were over 130,000 Morris Travellers out on the roads in 1970. Frustratingly every single one of the drivers had cast-iron alibis. The police scratched their heads and said they couldn't understand why this lead hadn't led to the killer. They stubbornly refused to admit that the witness had been mistaken and that they had wasted hundreds of hours of investigation time on a case of mistaken identity.

David Pollard was scathing of the police investigation into Barbara's murder. In 2014 David Pollard spoke with writer Chris Clark and talked rather bitterly about the decision to put so much time and effort into the Morris Traveller line of enquiry, *"The massive hunt for the Morris Traveller and its driver, which, as best it is possible to see, entirely misdirected. This skewed the whole of the investigation and perhaps a number of others. Where is there evidence in the presumed sighting with the Morris Travellers in Kimberley? If there is a plausible scenario for this, I haven't been able to find it. Setting off at maybe 8.30 in the morning, it doesn't take a pretty young woman hitching on a busy motorway in bright daylight until after four o'clock in the afternoon to travel 120 miles. Even if there were to be some explanation for this... It is well-nigh impossible that the Kimberley sighting was Barbara. There were no faggots in her stomach contents, only the breakfast she had before leaving home. But this supposed and highly publicised sighting certainly gave the murderer a clear run. Public attention was directed to the wrong time, the wrong place, the wrong vehicle and the wrong photofit."*

Notwithstanding the controversy over the Morris Traveller enquiry, the scope of the investigation into Barbara Mayo's murder was huge. Indeed, it was said to be the biggest single murder enquiry undertaken by any police force in the UK up to that time. At its height, 1500 police officers were involved, 126,000 people were interviewed, 47,000 statements were taken, the whereabouts and alibis of over 28,000 criminals (mostly sex offenders) were checked out, and 76,000 leads were followed. Despite all these efforts, the case went slowly cold.

In 1991 a cold case review of Jacqueline Ansell Lamb's murder was carried out by Cheshire Police conducted by Detective Superintendent Lawrence Mellor. In 1970 a link between Jacqueline's murder and Barbara Mayo's was briefly considered and dismissed. Now, Cheshire police re-examined the possible link between the two cases and noticed properly for the first time the startling similarities between the two murders. Then, new forensic methods of testing evidence which had not been available in the 1970s were utilised, and these tests finally proved beyond any doubt that the two cases were linked. For the first time, Cheshire and Derbyshire Constabularies came together in a joint cold case task force to re-investigate the murders.

As part of the 1991 cold case review, a major piece was prepared for the Crimewatch UK television programme—a large part of this reconstruction of events focused on the Morris Traveller line of enquiry. This seemed very peculiar, given that every driver of a Morris Traveller in the country had been cleared. However, Detective Superintendent David Doxley of Derbyshire Police clearly believed that the killer had been the driver of that Morris Traveller, and he told the Crimewatch viewers, "*I know some people chose to mislead us years ago, especially in relation to alibis. I am not interested in pursuing legal action against people who, for one reason or another, chose to mislead us all those years ago. Our main aim is to catch the killer. I don't believe that only the killer has the identity of the person responsible for Barbara's death.*"

Going down the same dead-end leads again got the cold case investigation nowhere. Despite the high-profile nature of the appeals, the joint investigation once again ground to a halt exactly as the original two investigations had in 1970.

There was no further progress with the case until 1997 when a further cold case review uncovered hitherto untraceable DNA evidence on an item of Barbara Mayo's clothing. There were exceedingly high hopes that this new evidence would lead to the killer finally being captured. The DNA was fed into the National DNA Database, which holds the DNA of over 200,000 convicted criminals. There was no match. Two hundred fifty old suspects were brought in, and DNA samples were taken. There was no match. Like everything else, the DNA evidence proved a frustrating investigative dead end.

In recent years there have been attempts to link the murders of Jacqueline Ansell-Lamb and Barbara Mayo to Peter Sutcliffe, the infamous Yorkshire Ripper[iii]. Most notably, Chris Clark and Tim Tate, in their 2015 book '*Yorkshire Ripper: The Secret Murders*' put forwards what, on the face of it, appears to be a convincing case for Peter Sutcliffe having been the killer of Jacqueline and Barbara. However, in 2020 Derbyshire Police confirmed that Peter Sutcliffe's DNA had been in the National DNA Database when the sample of DNA retrieved from Barabara Mayo's clothing was run through the database in 1997. So, Peter Sutcliffe *could not* have been Jacqueline or Barbara's killer. Despite this, there is still a stubbornly held belief by some that Jacqueline and Barbara are unaccounted victims of Peter Sutcliffe and that there is a dark and nebulous conspiracy to keep the truth from the public.

The publication of '*Yorkshire Ripper: The Secret Murders*' and its claims of previously unsuspected ripper murders garnered a lot of publicity and press excitement. It led to an understandably bitter David Pollard giving an interview to ITV News about the Ansell-Lamb/Mayo case. Pollard stated that it was his firm conviction that the murders had gone unsolved due to a mixture of police incompetence and then a cover-up to try and hide the mistakes and mishandling of the case.

In recent years a new theory has surfaced. This posits that on the day of both murders, Manchester City had been playing away, and both fixtures took place in London. The theory, therefore, took hold that the killer was a deranged Manchester City fan. However, in 1970 the police did try and follow this lead when investigating Barbara Mayo's murder. Whilst they found it nigh on impossible to account for every Manchester City fan who had attended the match, they felt that the theory was worthless, as the Manchester City fans would most likely have taken the M6 to return to Manchester and not the M1.

I have a terrible feeling that the murders of Jacqueline Ansell-Lamb and Barbara Mayo will now forever go unsolved. It's that most frustrating of cases where the truth just seems to be forever within reach but never close enough to touch. Indeed, in early 2023 the Bedfordshire Police, for reasons unknown, stated that they weren't satisfied with the earlier forensic results and now doubted that the murders were linked. I say they undoubtedly are. The psychology of the killer, the modus operandi and the scenes of the murders were far too similar for the cases not to be linked. Through it all, the twists and turns, the mistakes and blunders, I keep thinking of the victims—two innocent young girls who just wanted to get somewhere safely. Picked up, raped and murdered in lonely, isolated spots. It's truly the stuff of nightmares.

The Dating Game Killer: Cornelia Crilly, Ellen Hover, Jill Barcomb, Georgia Wixted, Charlotte Lamb, Jill Parenteau and Robin Samsoe

"Rodney Alcala may be the most dangerous of all of the killers that have ever been caught." –**Rex Julian Beaber, Attorney and Forensic Psychologist.**

To the Orange County Sheriff's Department, Rodney Alcala is known as *"The Monster."* He is more popularly known as 'The Dating Game Killer' to the wider public thanks to his appearance on the popular American game show. His friends and family knew him as Rod or even John. Officially, Alcala murdered six women and one twelve-year-old child. Unofficially, it's suspected by police and prosecutors that he may have murdered hundreds of women during the 1960s and 1970s. Rodney Alcala operated in a time before DNA, before CCTV, and before our mobile phones tracked our movements. Alcala lived in a time that made it relatively easy to be a serial killer and amass large numbers of victims without fear of detection or incarceration. He was also aided by his good looks and oodles of charm, very much akin to that other more famous contemporaneous serial killer, Ted Bundy. Despite only having good old-fashioned flat-footed police work at their disposal, it was still a case filled with missed opportunities by law enforcement agencies to catch Alcala and bad decisions made by correctional facilities, parole officers, employers and ordinary people. The type of decisions that will make you shake your head and realise that the past really was a different place.

Rodrigo Jacques Alcala Buquor was born on Monday the 23rd of August 1943, in San Antonio, Texas. Known to his friends and loved ones as Rodney, he was the third of four children born to Raoul and Anna Marie Alcala Buquor (nee Gutierrez). The family was reasonably well off, and after attending St Joseph Catholic Elementary School, Alcala was privately educated at Mount Sacred Heart. He was a studious child identified early as having an above-average IQ and consistently achieved above-average grades throughout his schooling. There were none of the red flags we would usually see in the childhood of a serial killer, no physical or sexual abuse, no head injuries, no bed-wetting or animal cruelty. Alcala had a nice, happy childhood and was seemingly normal and well-adjusted.

In 1953, the family moved to Mexico. Alcala's maternal grandmother had told the family that she was dying and wanted to spend her final months in her homeland. However, the wily old grandmother seemed to rally once the Alcala's had relocated to Mexico. Her final months became final years. Once again, Alcala attended private school whilst in Mexico, where he continued to be a star pupil. Somewhat annoyed by his mother-in-law's stubborn refusal to die, Raoul abandoned his family and returned to America, never to see any of them again. Dr Elizabeth Yardley believes that this was a key event in Alcala's life, *"I think that's quite a significant thing. I think that Alcala's relationship with his father was quite an important one to him, and I think that's something that stayed with Alcala throughout his life. I think it does feed into his offending behaviour."*

In 1956, Grandma finally died, and the family left Mexico and settled in Los Angeles. Alcala continued to be educated privately, first at St Alphonsus Elementary School and then at Cantwell-Sacred Heart of Mary High School. In his final year of high school, Alcala found the religious dogma of a catholic school to be somewhat suffocating. He, therefore, petitioned his mother to be allowed to attend an agnostic public school. At first, his mother was resistant, but when it became clear that Alcala was very unhappy at Cantwell, she enrolled him at Montebello High. Alcala attended the far less prestigious school for six months before his graduation. Despite the short time he was there, he threw himself straight into school activities, taking over the running of the School Yearbook Planning Committee and becoming a star cross-country runner for the school. He graduated as one of the top students in the school.

Alcala was popular with his fellow classmates. He had an easy-going charm, and his Hispanic good looks made him quite the hit with the female students. Alcala had the world at his feet. He had the winning combination of good looks, super intelligence and charm that could have taken him anywhere he wanted to go in life. With the world at his feet, Alcala decided to follow in his older brother's footsteps and enlist in the army.

On Monday the 19th of June 1961, Alcala signed up and was shipped out to Fort Bragg in North Carolina to train as a paratrooper. Alcala wasn't as good a soldier as he had been a student. A psychological report noted that Alcala was manipulative and vindictive. He also garnered a reputation for insubordination and was relegated to the position of a storeroom clerk. Then, in 1962, Raoul Alcala Buquor died, and after this, Alcala's poor attitude worsened. He performed tasks poorly and was reprimanded by his superiors several times. There were even allegations of sexual misconduct and rumours that Alcala was "*a sexual deviant.*"

On Friday the 22nd of February 1963, Alcala was awaiting a citation for dereliction of duty when he went Absent Without Leave (AWOL). Alcala made his way to New York City. Whilst hiding out in the city, Alcala got drunk and followed a young lady out of a bar, and a short distance down the street, he struck her over the head with a Coke bottle. Luckily, the young lady was only stunned and managed to run away. On Wednesday the 6th of March 1963, Alcala eventually handed himself in to military authorities at Fort McArthur and was returned to Fort Bragg. Here, he was dealt with by court-martial and demoted from Specialist Fourth Class (Corporal) to Private First Class. Many believe these events can be pinpointed as the start of Alcala's terrible crimes. As Dr Elizabeth Yardley explained, "*I think this is the period he starts, perhaps fantasising. His offending starts to take shape in his mind, if not in reality.*"

Then, in 1964, Alcala went AWOL again. He stole a car and a credit card and made his way from Fort Bragg to Los Angeles. He took a rather circumiclutious route. Alcala made his way to Myrtle Beach, South Carolina, where the military police apprehended him. However, as he was being transported back to Fort Campbell, he was able to give his military escorts the slip as they boarded a busy train.

Upon arriving in Los Angeles, Alcala's mother realised that the military police would be searching for her son, and she persuaded him to turn himself in.

However, before he did so, Alcala exposed his erect penis to his young sister, causing her to break down into wild hysterical crying. Alcala would later state that he was confused about his feelings towards his sister and "*did not know if he wanted to have sexual relations with her.*"

Alcala claimed that he wasn't responsible for his recent actions as he'd suffered a nervous breakdown. He was admitted into an Army hospital at Ford Ord in San Francisco before being transferred to El Toro Marine Corps Base to receive specialist psychiatric treatment. Army psychiatrists diagnosed Alcala as suffering from "*a chronic and severe antisocial personality... manifested by extreme hyper-irritability and inability to express organised and socially acceptable feelings of aggression and other emotions, impulsive and immature judgement and behaviour, absence of guilt in the presence of repeated acts of illegal and socially unacceptable aggressive nature and absence of... loyalty to persons, groups or codes.*"

Along with the damning psychiatric report, the psychiatrist also formalised Alcala's IQ for the first time. He was assessed as having an IQ of 135, placing him at the very top of the IQ scale. This is formally known as having a 'superior intellect,' but what you and I might call a genius-level IQ. After weeks of psychiatric assessment, Alcala was assessed as "*totally unsuitable for further military duty*" but was allowed an honourable discharge.

Returning to live with his mother at Monterey Park, Alcala enrolled at the University of California. Shortly after enrolling, he transferred to the prestigious University of California Los Angeles campus, where he read fine arts. Whilst in the army, Alcala developed a love of photography, which became his primary form of artistic expression. Just like when he was in school, Alcala became a popular and well-liked student at the university. He was adored on campus by both his fellow students and lecturers. Several of his tutors thought of him as a friend more than a student. In 1968, Alcala graduated with his bachelor's degree in fine art.

We don't know precisely when Rodney Alcala's sexual offending began. What we can say with 100% certainty is that by the time he graduated from UCLA, he was indulging in perverted and paedophilic sexual practices and had amassed quite a collection of pornographic photographs of underaged children. This all came to light on Wednesday the 25th of September 1968, when Alcala abducted eight-year-old Talia Shapiro as she walked along Sunset Strip. It was a blisteringly hot morning, and Talia was making her way to school on Gardner Street from the Chateau Marmont Hotel, where she lived with her music executive father. Talia would later say that she vividly remembers wearing a white dress that her grandmother had crocheted especially for her. With some unwarranted guilt, Talia felt that she needed to explain her actions that morning. When Alcal pulled up alongside Talia, he told her that her father had sent her and he was to give her a lift to school. Talia explained that she had been raised to respect her elders, and so she obeyed the instructions to get in the car.

As Alcala enticed the little girl into his vehicle, he was witnessed by a motorist called Donald Haines. Haines had a peculiar sixth sense that something wasn't right about the situation, and he took the unusual step of tailing Alcala to his apartment on De Longpre Avenue and then telephoned the police from a nearby phone box.

Officer Chris Camacho was dispatched. Camacho went over to the apartment. Camacho immediately felt that there was something nefarious afoot when he noted that Alcala had removed the licence plates from his car so that it would be almost impossible to identify. Alcala answered the door naked, "*I will always remember that face at the door*," Camacho would later say, "*A very evil face.*" Alcala told Camacho that he had just gotten out of the shower. This didn't ring true, as Alcala wasn't in the least bit wet. Camacha ordered Alcala to let him into the apartment. Alcala replied that he would after he put some trousers on. Alcala closed the door and didn't come back. Camacha realised something was desperately wrong, so he kicked in the door.

Talia lay naked, bound and gagged on the kitchen floor. She had been brutally raped and beaten, and she had received a vicious head injury from a dumbbell that Alcala had then placed over the child's throat in an attempt to choke her to death. The kitchen floor was awash with blood, "*There was more blood than you could imagine could be in an eight years old*," Camacha would later say. A camera set up on a tripod indicated that Alcala had taken photographs of the poor, petrified girl as he beat and defiled her.

Alcala had fled. As soon as he heard the front door being kicked in, he bolted out of the back door completely stark naked. Camacha had a choice: he could chase the suspect or stay and comfort the little girl. He chose to stay and comfort the girl.

A young detective by the name of Steve Hodel[iv] was put in charge of the case. He quickly put a name to the man responsible for Talia's rape and attempted murder. Alcala had fled, leaving behind his student pass from UCLA. Hodel also found hundreds of sexually explicit photographs of young girls and boys, seemingly all taken by Alcala.

In an attempt to try to track Alcala down, Hodel went to speak with Alcala's friends, family, and lecturers at UCLA. Hodel discovered that Alcala was "*a snake charmer*" who had beguiled everyone he had ever met. Everyone thought he was "*a great guy*," with one lecturer insisting to Hodel that there must have been a mistake as Alcala "*wouldn't hurt anybody*."

Rodney Alaca went on the run. He changed his name to John Berger and moved to New York, where he enrolled in New York University's School of Arts to read filmmaking. This easy changing between identities was key to how Rodney Alcala was able to get away with his crimes for so long, "*He cleverly evades detection while simultaneously establishing new personas to introduce to those he meets,*" Dr Elizabeth Yardley explained, "*Like a snake, he sheds his skin and adopts fresh identities, which is how I would describe his approach*." Earle Robitaille, the retired chief of Huntington Beach Police, agrees with this assessment, "*He's a confidence man in that respect. His ultimate body count will be dependent upon his ability to con children, adults, mostly women but probably some males somewhere along the line, into believing that he is whatever he's attempting to make them believe he is at that moment.*"

In New York, Alcala studied under the famed but problematic director Roman Polanski. Alaca became well-liked by both the other students and lecturers. He dated several women and spent a lot of time in the hip and trendy Greenwich Village district. As always, his grades placed him in the top percentile of students. He worked part-time as a security guard, and in July 1969, he secured a summer job as a counsellor at 'New Beginnings,' an all-girls art and drama camp based in Georges Mills, New Hampshire. Alcala helped out at the camp every summer until 1971.

Cornelia Crilley was a New Yorker born and raised. She grew up in a large and very close Catholic family in Queens. She attended All Saints Commerical High School in Brooklyn with a dream of becoming an air stewardess. She took on a job as a clerical assistant at Jacobs, Persinger and Parker law firm, hoping to save up enough money to attend flight attendant school. Whilst working at Jacobs, Persinger and Parker, Cornelia met a young lawyer by the name of Leon Borstein, and they fell in love.

Cornelia eventually temporarily left New York to attend the Trans World Airlines (TWA) flight attendant school in Overland Park, Kansas. Here, Cornelia not only learned the basics of being a flight attendant, such as emergency protocols and safety procedures, but she also had lessons on hairstyling, make-up tuition, deportment and weight management. Indeed, Cornelia had to step on the scales every week and prove to her teachers that she practised self-control and wasn't piling on the pounds. What did this have to do with serving people hot drinks and ensuring inflight comfort? Well, it was the 1970s, a time of rampant sexism, when flight attendants were meant to be objects of lust and desire and were derisively called in some circles 'trolly dollies'.

Upon graduating from flight attendant school, Cornelia returned to New York with two other newly qualified flight attendants, and they all rented an apartment on 43rd Street. Cornelia also rekindled her relationship with Leon Borstein. Cornelia enjoyed a jet-setting lifestyle of international travel and rubbing shoulders with celebrities on internal flights from New York to Los Angeles.

On Saturday the 12th of June 1971, Cornelia moved with her two friends to a new apartment at 427 83rd Street in the Yorkville district of New York. Cornelia's flatmates were both working that day, but Cornelia's flight had been cancelled due to a technical problem, and so she supervised the move. At around midday, Cornelia telephoned her mother to tell her that the removal men had dropped off all their belongings and that she was going to spend a few hours unpacking. Cornelia's mother said that she would phone back later that day to make sure that Cornelia was settled in okay.

When Cornelia's mother phoned later that afternoon, she got no reply. Mrs Crilley kept calling and kept getting no reply. By 5.00 p.m., she was very worried and so telephoned Leon Borstein at the offices of Jacobs, Persinger and Parker. Leon promised to check on Cornelia on his way home from work. When he got to the apartment, he got no reply. So, he went to the local police station, where he knew several of the local beat cops, and one of them agreed to help Leon break into the apartment.

They found Cornelia lying on the bed. She was naked from the waist up, and her bra had been roughly shoved into her mouth to gag her. Cornelia had been raped and beaten. The killer had savagely bitten her left breast and strangled Cornelia both manually and with her tights. Alcala had a very unique method of killing his victims. Forensic psychologist Rex Julian Beaber highlighted the horrid method in vivid detail, "(Alcala) *would strangle them to the point of near death and then allow them to be revived, strangle them to the point of death, allow them to be returned to life, and then finally at some point to kill them. A man who got his sexual excitement and arousal from being right there at the precipice of life and death. He needs to see the fire of terror in the woman's eyes as he's on the verge of snuffing out her soul for him to be aroused.*"

Cornelia's murder became national news, not least because TWA put forward a $5,000 reward and the Professional Airline Stewards Association stumped up a further $1,000. Leon was the immediate suspect; he was interviewed five times by the police, but when his Jacobs, Persinger and Parker colleagues gave him a cast iron alibi, the police moved on to consider the apartment's handyman. He, too, proved to have a solid alibi. The case seemed to fizzle out. Cornelia became just another of the 2000 murders that plagued New York that dreadful year, and for decades, it looked like Cornelia's murder would be a lasting mystery until science reached a point where traces of Alcala's DNA could be extracted from samples taken from the bitemark left in Cornelia's breast.

On Wednesday the 11th of August 1971, two female students from the New Beginnings summer camp visited the local Post Office. Here, their eyes fell upon a list of the FBI's ten most wanted criminals. They were shocked to see a photograph of one of their counsellors, the man they knew as John Berger. They reported the finding to the camp's director, who went to check out the wanted poster for himself. Although the poster was for Rodney Alcala, the corresponding photograph clearly showed the man the director knew as John Berger. So, the director called the FBI.

The next day, FBI agents arrested Alcala and took him to Boston for processing. Steve Hodel was notified and immediately jumped on a plane from Los Angeles to Boston. Hodel found Alacala to be sly, calculating and manipulative, *"He was kind of low key, a bit introverted, but I could see his mind functioning, and that's what made this guy so dangerous. He was able to read people very well and stay a step or two or three ahead of them. For him, it was all kind of a chess game."* When Hodel attempted to question Alcala about Talia Shapiro, Alcala replied, *"I want to forget all about that. I don't want to talk about Rod Alcala and what he did."*

By the time Rodney Alcala came to face trial for the attempted murder and rape of Talia Shapiro, there was a problem. The Shapiro family no longer lived in the United States. Talia had been in a coma for thirty-two days, but luckily, she had made a full recovery. Her family were deeply traumatised by the whole sickening event, and they took the decision to return to Puerto Vallarta, Mexico. Without Talia's testimony, the prosecutors were worried that the case would flounder. So, they offered Alcala a plea deal. Instead of facing trial for kidnap, rape and attempted murder, Alcala could plead to a single charge of child molestation. In return, he would receive an indeterminate sentence. No minimum term would be set. It would be up to Alcala to prove to a parole board that he was safe to be released back into society. Alcala took the deal. On Friday the 19th of May 1972, Alcala started his prison sentence.

Rodney Alcala served just three years imprisonment for the murderous attack on Talia Shapiro. By August 1974, Alcala had persuaded the prison psychiatrist that he no longer posed a danger to the public, a glowing report was put before the parole board, and he was released. As a term of his parole, he had to sign on as a registered sex offender.

Upon release, Alcala returned to live with his mother. He wasn't out of trouble long. On Thursday the 17th of October 1974, Alcala abducted thirteen-year-old Julie Johnson from a service station. He drove her to Huntington Beach, where he forced Julie to smoke a marijuana joint with him before sexually assaulting her. Julie's screams attracted the attention of a Park Ranger who came to her rescue.

Alcala was initially charged with kidnapping, supplying drugs to a minor and violating the terms of his parole. By the time the case got to court on Thursday the 26th of December 1974, the kidnapping charge had been dropped. Alcala pleaded guilty to the two lesser charges and was returned to custody. Alcala spent a further two years in prison before being rereleased in December 1976.

In June 1977, Rodney Alcala petitioned his parole officer for special dispensation to leave the state of California and travel across the country to New York. He said he wanted to visit friends there. Unusually, for a registered sex offender who was a known flight risk and who had already breached the terms of his parole, Alcala was given permission to make the trip. Rodney Alcala travelled to New York in July 1977.

Ellen Jane Hover was twenty-three years old and came from a well-to-do family. Her parents were Hermon and Yvonne Josette Ealy Hover. Hermon Hover was a famed Hollywood nightclub owner, and Yvonne had been a beautiful and much-desired showgirl. Ellen grew up around celebrities. Her parents counted Frank Sinatra, Jerry Lewis, Cary Grant, Jimmy Stewart, Lucille Ball and Judy Garland among their close personal friends. Ellen's godfathers were Rat Pack members Dean Martin and Sammy Davies Jr. Despite growing up around Hollywood royalty, Ellen was entirely grounded, *"Ellen was especially – almost heartbreakingly – sweet,"* her cousin/stepsister[v] would later say. It was this type of sweetness that Alcala was adept at manipulating; as Dr Elizabeth Yardley highlights, "(Alcala is) *a very accomplished predator, he sniffs out his prey, identifies their vulnerabilities and moves in for the kill."*

Stories of Ellen's kindness abound. When Ellen's best friend, Nina, wasn't asked to their High School Prom by anyone, Ellen politely turned down the offer from the boy she had always fancied from afar so that she could be Nina's date. When another friend found herself disowned by her deeply religious family after falling pregnant out of wedlock, Ellen dropped all her plans. She moved in with the friend for several weeks so that she could help attend to the new mother and look after the newborn baby.

Ellen attended Beaver College, Pennsylvania, where she minored in music and majored in biology. Ellen was a gifted pianist but ultimately planned on attending medical school to follow in her stepfather's footsteps and become a neurosurgeon. After graduating college, Ellen moved to New York to be closer to her mother and stepfather, renting an apartment at 686 3rd Avenue in midtown Manhattan. The apartment was hardly luxurious. Indeed, when Ellen moved in, the apartment was run down and had been cut off by the electricity board.

On Wednesday the 13th of July 1977, Ellen was seen by her friend Alan Cohen standing outside her apartment talking to a good-looking young man with long curly hair tied into a ponytail. Ellen told friends that the man was a photographer whom she'd met at the local Unemployment Office. The mysterious man had told Ellen that he had a fine art degree from UCLA, had studied under Roman Polanski and had recently returned to New York after being a counsellor at a summer camp in New Hampshire. He had organised a photo shoot with Ellen by the Hudson River, after which he had been "*pressuring her to have lunch with him.*" Alan Cohen saw the same man entering Ellen's apartment two days later. Later that evening, Ellen failed to meet friends with whom she had arranged a dinner date. Ellen also failed to make a scheduled call to her mother the following day.

The police were called, and Detective Donald Tasik was placed in charge of the investigation. He searched Ellen's apartment. Nothing was missing or out of place. However, in her appointment diary for Friday the 15th of July 1977, Ellen had noted an appointment with "*John Berger- Photographer.*"

On Wednesday the 14th of December 1977, Detective Tasik became aware that Rodney Alcala had used the alias John Berger whilst on the run for the rape and attempted murder of Talia Shapiro. Tasik went to question Alcala. To Tasik's surprise, Alcala readily admitted that he had known Ellen Hover and was indeed the John Berger mentioned in her appointment diary. Tasik asked Alcala if he would take a polygraph, but Alcala refused. Unfortunately, Tasik had nothing else to go on. Nothing linked Rodney Alcala to an actual crime, so Tasik had to let Alcala go. After hitting this investigative brick wall, Tasik didn't just quietly shelve the investigation. He called in the Federal Bureau of Investigation, but even they couldn't make any headway with the case.

In June 1978, Detective Tasik was made aware that Rodney Alcala had a specific spot favoured when studying at New York University's School of Arts and taking photographs for his portfolio. It was some thirty miles north of New York City in Tarrytown, Westchester County. So, Tasik made a concerted effort to search every inch of the land. Ellen's body was finally found hidden in a shallow grave under some rocks. She had been buried on land owned by the Rockefeller family overlooking the Hudson River. The body was so severely decomposed identification was only possible with reference to dental records and some jewellery. It was impossible for pathologists to discern how Ellen had died. No valuable forensic evidence had survived the near year-long exposure to the shifting elements of New York weather.

Despite the fact that Detective Tasik, his colleagues, and the FBI strongly believed that Rodney Alcala murdered Ellen Hover, for the moment, they just didn't have the evidence that they could place before a jury and prove the case. They were forced to file Ellen's murder away as an unsolved crime.

When Alcala returned to Los Angeles on Sunday the 31st of July 1977, he secured a job as a typesetter at the Los Angeles Times. Many people, such as writer and researcher Stella Sands, have expressed incredulity that such an auspicious organisation would have hired a registered sex offender, *"You have to put this into perspective,"* Sands said, *"On the lam for three years, ten most wanted, two stints in jail, felon, he applies under his own name, Rodney Alcala, and he gets the job."* Once again, Alcala proved to be charming and easily made friends at the much-lauded organisation. Alcala's photography portfolio impressed many of the reporters and photographers at the newspaper. Despite the fact that many of his photographs were of partially clothed young children, Alcala's new friends simply put this down to Alcala being artsy.

Jill Barcomb was just eighteen. She was originally from Oneida, Madison County. The daughter of Maurice and Joyce Barcomb, she was one of eleven children born to devoutly catholic parents. Jill's auntie described her as *"a bubbly little girl"* but with *"a wild side."* Jill dropped out of Oneida High School and started to accrue a few juvenile convictions for petty offences. Her parents were furious, and rather than face their rancour, she decided to move out of the family home and live with her big sister.

Jill made it clear that she wasn't happy in sleepy little Onedia. She wanted to head to Hollywood and find fame and fortune. So, in October 1977, Jill hitchhiked her way to Los Angeles. She did this without telling her parents or wider family of her intentions. Jill's parents reported her disappearance to the police, but as far as the authorities were concerned, Jill was just another unhappy teenage runaway.

Jill lasted less than a month in the big city. On Thursday the 10th of Nover 1977, police were called to the discovery of a body on a dirt track off Franklin Canyon Road, close to the famed Hollywood Hills sign and Marlon Brando's home. Jill was found naked and positioned on all fours. Her neck was broken, and her head had been awkwardly positioned so that it was tucked down, her chin touching the top of her breasts and the top of her head resting on the ground. Her right hand had been tucked under the body, which caused her backside to thrust upwards into the air. Jill had been raped both anally and vaginally. The killer had also bitten her breast, and there were burn marks on the body. Her face was so mutilated that her family could not recognise her when asked to carry out the identification. Jill had been beaten and strangled with the leg of her own trousers and belt. One of the weapons used to beat Jill had been a rock, which was found soaked in blood and discarded close to the body. Footprints behind Jill's body indicated that whoever killed her had stood close behind Jill's body and taken photographs. Her brother, Bruce Barcomb, would later lament, "*It wasn't just murder, it wasn't just rape, it was brutal, it was sadistic.*"

Georgia Wixted was a twenty-seven-year-old orthopaedic oncology nurse at Centinela Hospital in Inglewood, California. She was born on Thursday the

22nd of December 1949, in Troy, Rensselaer County, New York. She was one of two children born to Matthew and Mary Wixted (nee Golden). Her parents separated when Georgia was five, and Mary took Georgia to live in Los Angeles. Matthew Wixted died after a short illness when Georgia was eleven. At roughly the same time as her father's death, Georgia also fell gravely ill and spent a considerable time in hospital. During this period, Georgia decided she wanted to be a nurse.

On the morning of Saturday 17th of December 1977, Georgia Wixted had arranged to collect a co-worker called Barbara Gale and drive them both to Centinela Hospital. Georgia failed to collect Barabara and didn't turn up for her shift. Concerned, her boss called the police and Officers Jack Nenninger and Mike Powers were dispatched to Georgia's ocean-view apartment in Malibu. They immediately noticed that a screen had been removed from one of the ground-floor windows, the window had been forced open, and a box had been placed beneath the open window. A footmark on top of the box indicated that someone had used it to climb up through the window. The front door to the apartment had been unlocked from the inside.

Inside, the house was in darkness and stiflingly hot. Georgia was discovered lying on her back on the bedroom floor. Prosecutor Matt Murphy would later say of Georgia's murder, "*The viciousness and sadism involved in her murder is so disturbing and so profound.*" Georgia's legs were bent at the knees framing her bloodied vagina. She was completely naked and was covered in bruises and lacerations. Her head was one giant open wound. Her skull had been '*ripped open*' using the claw end of a clawhammer. Her arm was fractured and dislocated. She had been raped orally and vaginally and strangled with her own knickers. Blood-covered bedsheets, a duvet, a pillow and a nightie surrounded the body. Two feet from the body lay the blood-covered claw hammer. Blood spatter covered the bedrest, floor and walls. In the bathroom was a blood-covered soap bar that the killer had used to try and clean themselves before leaving the scene. In the kitchen sink, a blood-covered towel was found discarded.

Lieutenant Philip Bullington of the LA County Sherriff's Department was placed in charge of the investigation, but despite his best efforts, he was never able to make any headway with the investigation, and it quickly hit one investigative dead end after another. Much to Bullington's frustration, the case became an unsolvable mystery.

Charlotte Lamb was a thirty-two-year-old mature student at Santa Monica College. To pay her way through college, she secured a legal secretary job. On Friday the 23rd of June 1978, Charlotte invited some friends to join her at a new Santa Monica nightclub called Moody's. Her friends declined the invitation, and so Charlotte decided to go to the nightclub alone.

On Saturday the 24th of June 1978, Zaffar Shah walked into the laundry room at 617 Illinois Court, Segunda. He found the body of a naked woman lying on her back with her legs spread wide apart and her arms positioned under her torso so that her breasts heaved outwards. Psychologist Dr Veronica Thomas would later say that the posing of the body was trying to send a message to law enforcement. It was the killer saying, *"I am here. You will remember me."* Blood marks on the front of the body indicated that the victim had been initially lying on her stomach before the killer had turned the body over and positioned the body so that whoever found it received the maximum shock and felt the maximum horror. The woman had been badly beaten and raped. There was blunt force trauma to the back of her head, a bite mark on her breast and shoulder, and lacerations to her genitals. She had been strangled with a shoelace.

William Gaynor of the LA County Sherriff's Department was placed in charge of the investigation. He interviewed all of the building's residents, the building manager and his wife. No one knew the victim; she had to be categorised as a Jane Doe. How she came to be in the laundry room was a complete mystery.

Later that same day, police gave a parking ticket to Charlotte's Datsun car. Its ticket had expired in a parking garage on 4th Street, a block from Moody's nightclub. Over the next few days, Charlotte's friends became increasingly worried as she didn't return their calls. She also failed to attend her work and didn't phone in sick. Her car also failed to move, and it was eventually towed away. On Wednesday the 28th of June 1978, Charlotte was finally reported missing, and it didn't take the police long to connect the missing young woman with the murdered woman found in the laundry room at 617 Illinois Court.

On Wednesday the 13th of September 1978, Rodney Alcala took part in the television show, which led to his receiving the nickname 'The Dating Game Killer[vi]'. The premise of the show was relatively simple. The three eligible bachelors would hide behind a screen and would be asked increasingly flirty and sexual innuendo-laced questions by a contestant seeking love. Based on their answers, the contestant would then pick which eligible bachelor she wanted to go on an all-expenses-paid date with. How a registered sex offender currently on parole for rape and kidnap was allowed onto such a nationally syndicated gameshow is beggar's belief. The producers would later admit that nobody ever thought of carrying out background checks on the contestants.

Mike Metzger, the producer of the Dating Game, didn't initially like Rodney Alcala. He said he found him creepy and turned down Alcala's application to be on the show. However, several female production staff, including Metzger's wife, Ellen, persuaded Mike to let Alcala be a contestant on the show, as the females found Alcala to be very charming and attractive. As usual, when the cameras started rolling, Alcala was witty and charming, and he easily won the date with the contestant.

The female contestant's name was Cheryl Bradshaw, a drama teacher from Phoenix, Arizona. After the programme was recorded, Alcala and Cheryl were introduced properly in the green room, where Contestant Coordinator Ellen Metzger arranged their date. They were to go on a rollercoaster ride at Magic Mountain Theme Park and then have tennis lessons.

Backstage, Jed Mills, one of the other contestants on the show, took an instant dislike to Alcala, "*The vibes I got from him while we were doing the show and backstage, and even while we were doing the actual filming, were not good vibes. There was something wrong with this guy... He had an attitude like he knew better than everyone else...thinking back on it, it was very spooky... horrible.*" Alcala was so obnoxious and became so confrontational with the other male contestants that things got a little heated between Jed and Alcala. At one point, they nearly came to blows, and they had to be separated by production staff. Alcala then sat brooding in the corner, muttering discontentedly under his breath.

It seems that this view wasn't just sour grapes on Jed's behalf, as he wasn't the only one who got a bad vibe from Alcala. Contestant Coordinator Ellen Metzger would later say, "*At the audition, (Alcala) was charming and fun; at the recording, he changed. Everything he said to me was creepy, I really, from when I first (met) him to the taping, I couldn't look at the guy.*" The morning after recording the episode, Cheryl Bradshaw telephoned Ellen Metzger in a distraught state, "*She said, 'Ellen, I can't go out with this guy. There's weird vibes that are coming off of him. He's very strange. I am not comfortable. Is that going to be a problem?' And of course, I said, 'No,'*" It was then left to Ellen to telephone Alcala and break the bad news to him that his all-expenses-paid date was off.

On Tuesday the 13th of February 1979, fifteen-year-old Monique Hoyt was hitchhiking home to Pasadena when she was picked up by a good-looking dark-haired man who introduced himself as Rodney. Alcala told Monique that he was a professional photographer and asked if she would like to model for him. Monique agreed. They spent the night at Alcala's mother's house, and the following day, they drove to mountains outside Banning, eighty miles east of Los Angeles.

They found a wooded glade where Alcala took some pictures of Monique. Using all his charm, Alcala then persuaded Monique to pose naked. After taking the photographs, as Monique put her t-shirt back on, Alcala smashed her over the head with a tree branch. He then raped Monique both vaginally and analy and viciously bit her genitals. As Monique cried out in pain, Alcala stuffed her t-shirt into her mouth and then choked her to unconsciousness.

When Monique recovered consciousness, she discovered that Alcala had bound her hands and feet and was sitting beside her hysterically crying. Monique asked Alcala if he was okay. She then attempted to form a bond with him, told him that she really liked him and wanted to spend more time with him, and eventually was able to persuade him to untie her and take her back to his mother's house. On the drive back, Alcala stopped at a petrol station to use the bathroom. Monique made a run for it. She ran to a nearby motel, where she began screaming for help. A couple of motel guests helped Monique, taking her into the safety of their motel room, where they called the police, but by the time the police arrived, Alcala had fled.

Monique was taken to a police station, where her witness statement was taken. She was then shown a photographic lineup of known sex offenders. Without hesitation, Monique picked out Rodney Alcala. The following day Rodney Alcala was arrested at his mother's house for kidnap and rape. When questioned, Alcala initially stated that he and Monique had entered into consensual, if rough, sex. However, eventually, he dropped the charade and admitted that he had brutally raped the fifteen-year-old.

On Friday the 16th of March 1979, Alcala appeared before a judge. Mercurial as ever, Alcala had changed his mind about his guilt, and despite his earlier confession, he now stated that he was innocent of any wrongdoing. A trial was set for September of that year, and Alcala's mother posted $10,000 bail for her son.

Alcala had some difficult explaining to do at the Los Angeles Times. He hadn't been at work for nearly a month, and no one had contacted them to explain why. He didn't intend to tell his bosses at the esteemed publication that he had been held on remand for raping a child and instead handed in his notice telling them that his photography business was taking off.

Despite the impending prosecution, Alcala also started to date a lady called Elizabeth Kelleher, whom he met in a bar. They spent most days together, and Elizabeth encouraged Alcala's photography. On days they didn't see each other, Alcala would telephone Elizabeth and spend hours talking to her on the phone. It seemed like a normal and healthy relationship for all intents and purposes. However, it obviously left Alcala unsatisfied.

Jill Parenteau was twenty-one, born on Thursday the 17th of October 1957, in Glendale, Los Angeles. She was reading business at Pasadena City College but had a part-time job as a computer programmer for Technbilt Ltd, based in Burbank. They had been so impressed by Jill's skills as a programmer and general work ethic that they offered her a full-time management position. A shrewd saver and spender, Jill owned a second-floor flat in an apartment complex on Peyton Avenue.

On Wednesday the 13th of June 1979, Jill went on a date with a former school friend called Dan Brady. They went to see a Dodgers game together. Brady had been smitten with Jill for a long time, and this was to be their first official date. All of Jill's family were excited about the date, as they believed that Jill and Dan were a perfect match for each other.

The next day, Jill didn't show up for work, and her co-workers were unable to get hold of her over the telephone. Concerned by the unusual behaviour, Jill's boss sent a coworker called Janet Jordan to Jill's apartment to see if Jill was alright.

Janet found the apartment unlocked. Jill was lying on her back on her bed. A lampshade had been partly covered with a bedsheet and angled so that a shaft of light fell upon Jill's body. Once again, the body had been posed. Pillows had been placed beneath her shoulders to prop Jill's body up, and her legs were splayed wide open. Jill had been badly beaten and raped orally, vaginally and analy. Death had been caused by strangulation, the killer using the flex of an electric blanket. A search of the building uncovered a window leading to the external patio that had been carefully removed, as had the insect screen covering it, and a lightbulb in one of the stairwells had been taken out.

Gordon Bowers from the LA County Sherriff's Department was placed in charge of the investigation. One of his first actions was to track down Dan Brady. Dan told Bowers that after the game, he had left Jill safe and well at her apartment. The programme from the Dodgers Game and a receipt for some drinks found in Jill's kitchen seemed to verify this alibi. Brady's roommates independently verified the time Brady arrived home. He just wouldn't have had enough time to drop Jill off after the game, rape and murder her and then drive home in time to say goodnight to his roommates. Bowers, therefore, deduced that whoever killed Janet must have been a complete stranger to her. He had probably broken into the apartment complex via the window, removed the bulb from the stairwell fitting, and loitered in the darkness until a suitable female resident was unlucky enough to use the stairwell.

Bowers was only partly right. Alcala had waited for Jill in the stairwell, but the crime had been very much targeted. It would only come to light much later that Rodney Alcala had known Jill Parenteau. They had met at a local drinking establishment that they both frequented called the Handlebar Saloon. After becoming drinking buddies, Alcala had asked Jill out on a date, but she had rebuffed him. Alcala just couldn't take the rejection. Alcala had subjected Jill to a barrage of obscene phone calls over a period of several months. Later investigation showed that the calls would stop whenever Alcala left town and would start again immediately upon his return. Alcala had targeted Jill simply because he couldn't stand the thought of a woman saying no to him.

Robin Christine Samsoe was just twelve years old and described as *"the most loving child a mother could have."* On Saturday the 20th of June 1979, Robin and her friend Bridget Wilvert went to Huntington Beach, Orange County, to spend a few blissful hours playing in the sun. As the two girls played on the beach, a good-looking young man with long curly hair approached them and asked if he could take the girl's photographs. Bridget would later describe him as *"like a shark in the water honing in on a seal."* It just so happened that

Bridget's neighbour, Jackye Young, was also sunbathing on the beach that day. She didn't like the look of the man who had approached the two little girls, and she interceded and shooed the man away. Jackye stayed with the girls for the rest of the morning and, later that afternoon, escorted them both home.

Robin was quite the canny little girl. Her parents couldn't afford to pay for the ballet lessons that Robin so desperately wanted. So, Robin had come to an arrangement with Mrs Fleming, the teacher at the local ballet school. At weekends and in school holidays, Robin would act as Mrs Flemings's unofficial secretary, answering phones and taking messages and such, and in return, Robin would receive free ballet lessons. At 3.10 p.m. that afternoon, Robin borrowed Bridget's bicycle to cycle to the ballet school and start her new Saturday job. Robin never arrived. Deeply concerned by Robin's non-appearance, Mrs Fleming telephoned Robin's auntie. With growing panic, the family began to telephone Robin's friends. When they realised that Robin was not with any of her friends or relatives, they telephoned the police.

Detective Craig Robinson was placed in charge of the missing person's case. He had Bridget Wilvert and Jackye Young help police sketch artist Marilyn Droz draw a composite sketch of the photographer who had tried to take pictures of the two girls. The sketch was subsequently released to the press and received wide publicity.

Three important witnesses came forward, thanks to the sketch. The first was Police Officer Dennis McNaughton, who had been involved in the Monique Hoyt case. He told Robinson that the sketch looked exactly like a convicted sex offender currently on parole called Rodney Alcala, with whom he had recently had dealings for raping a fifteen-year-old girl. The second was Rodney Alcala's parole officer. He also contacted the police to state that Alcala looked like the guy in the sketch and confirmed that Alcala was a registered sex offender. The third witness was dear old good Samaritan Donald Haines. He, too, put forward Rodney Alcala's name and told Robinson about how he had witnessed Rodney Alcala kidnap Talia Shapiro all those years before and how his quick thinking had saved the girl's life.

On Tuesday the 26th of June 1979, Detective Robinson retrieved Rodney Alcala's mugshot from police records and showed it to Bridget Wilvert and Jackye Young. They both confirmed that this was the man who had tried to take Robin and Bridget's photograph on Huntington Beach that fateful day.

Two officers, John Prchal and Michael Biggs, were tasked with surveilling Rodney Alcala. At first, they didn't recognise him, as he had cut his long hair and straightened his natural curls. Once they established Alcala's identity, they spent the next few days following him as he pootled around in his Datsun F-10 station wagon. However, somehow, Alcala realised he was being followed, and Prchal and Biggs lost Alcala several times as he would suddenly drive erratically, make sudden turns without indicating or suddenly accelerate away. The surveillance became a frustrating experience as the officers tried to second-guess Alcala's every move.

On Monday the 2nd of July 1979, Robin Samsoe's body was discovered in a remote ravine off Santa Anita Canyon Road, forty miles from where she was last seen. U.S. Forestry Service Firefighter William Poepke officially made the discovery. You might have noticed that I wrote there *officially discovered* because, bizarrely, although Poepke was the first to <u>report</u> the discovery of Robin's body, the discovery had actually been made almost two weeks before by one of Poepke's colleagues. At around 5.00 p.m. on the 20th of June, U.S. Forestry Service firefighter Dana Crappa was driving to work along Santa Anita Canyon Road. She had noticed a 1976 registration Datsun F-10 station wagon parked at the side of the road. A Hispanic-looking man with long, dark, curly hair was dragging a blonde-haired, pale-skinned little girl away from the vehicle towards the ravine at the side of the road.

As Crappa returned home from her shift later that night, she saw the same Datsun F-10 parked a little further along the road, and the same Hispanic, long, dark, curly-haired man sat resting on a rock not far away from the vehicle. Now, he was minus the little blonde girl. The man seemed grubby and dirty, with soil marks on his shirt.

Crappa instinctively felt that something had not been right about the man. In fact, she couldn't get the man and the struggling little girl out of her head. Unable to rest, she drove back to the scene later that night and began looking around with a flashlight. Crappa found Robin Samsoe's body dumped in the ravine but was too terrified to tell anyone. She left the scene and kept her mouth shut, telling no one about her gruesome discovery. This decision ultimately cost Crappa her job and ultimately pushed her to a psychological breakdown.

Establishing the body's identity took three days, and the medical examiner could only do so by referencing dental records. Robin's mother, Marianne Connelly, became frustrated and angry by how long this process took. She angrily asked how many other little girls with blonde hair had gone missing. Detective Robinson tearfully replied that they couldn't take the child's hair colour into account as there was no hair left on the badly decomposed cadaver.

Medical Examiner Sharon Schnittker carried out the autopsy. Unfortunately, due to the level of decomposition and partial animalisation of the corpse, she was unable to ascertain the cause of death or if Robin had been raped or sexually assaulted.

Meanwhile, Rodney Alcala drove 1300 miles to Seattle, Washington. Here, he rented a storage unit where he stored away several boxes. He then stayed the night in a motel before driving all the way back to Los Angeles. Upon his return, he told Elizabeth Kelleher that he was considering moving to Texas and he'd like her to accompany him. He told other friends that he was thinking of returning to Mexico. Whether Alcala was genuinely thinking of absconding to one of these destinations or just laying the groundwork for future excuses as to why he might be absent for a long period of time if he was to receive a prison sentence for raping Monique Hoyt, no one can really say.

On Tuesday the 24th of July 1979, the police arrested Rodney Alcala for Robin Samsoe's murder and executed a warrant on his mother's house. During the search, police found 1200 photographs of women and young children and the receipt for the storage unit in Seattle. Later that day, Alcala's sisters, Christine and Marie, went to visit Alcala in prison; unbeknown to them, their conversation was being recorded by the police. Alcala told his sisters about the storage unit in Seattle, and he ordered them to get rid of its contents as soon as they could.

Intrigued by this new information, the police went to a judge and obtained another search warrant for the storage locker. On Thursday the 26th of July 1979, Detective Robinson flew to Seattle to execute the warrant. Inside the lock-up, Robinson found what was later described as *"the motherload."* Amongst the lock-up's content was a silk pouch containing dozens of women's earrings, including a set of earrings belonging to Robin Samsoe and a pair that would later be linked to Charlotte Lamb via DNA. There were also over 1700 more photographs of women and young children, many of them pornographic.

On Saturday the 28th of July 1979, Alcala once again appeared in court for an arraignment hearing; he was charged with the murder of Robin Samsoe, kidnapping, robbery and lewd and lascivious behaviour with a child under the age of fourteen. This time, bail was set so high it would be impossible for his mother to pay. Unable to offer up $250,000, he was safely remanded into custody.

Whilst in custody, Alcala allegedly confessed to Robin's murder to three other inmates. This complicated the looming trial as the three inmates were now material witnesses in the case, and their lawyer had also been appointed to defend Alcala. This was a clear conflict of interest, so Alcala had to be appointed a new public defender. A young lawyer by the name of John Barnett was appointed to defend Alcala, and he immediately sought an adjournment of the trial so that he could become better acquainted with the case. The judge agreed to the adjournment, and the case was adjourned until Thursday the 4th of October 1979.

In the meantime, Alcala still faced trial for raping Monique Hoyt. When the trial arrived in September, this too was adjourned off as a psychiatrist had assed Monique as being too psychologically damaged by the horrendous experience to testify.

Rodney Alcala's trial for the murder of Robin Samsoe finally began in February 1980 before Judge Philp E. Schwab. It lasted over two and a half months, and fifty witnesses were called. The prosecutor described the trial as *"very long and very difficult."* Prosecutor Richard Farnell won an early victory when he had Judge Schwab rule that Alcala's previous convictions could be used to strengthen the case against Alcala. John Barnett was optimistic that he could still win an acquittal. The evidence against Alcala was entirely circumstantial. The only truly damning evidence against Alcala was his having been in possession of the earrings. It was alleged but not proved. Robin had been wearing it on the day she disappeared.

The jury retired to consider its verdict late on the afternoon of Tuesday the 29th of April 1980. They returned quickly on the morning of Wednesday the 30th of April 1980. They had deliberated for just two hours. They had found Rodney Alcala guilty of the kidnap and the first-degree murder of Robin Samsoe. The jury was then asked to consider Rodney Alcala's punishment: should Alcala face life imprisonment or the death penalty? The jury retired again, and, a week later, on Wednesday the 7th of May 1980, they returned to tell Judge Schwab that Rodney Alcala should face the death penalty for his dreadful crimes. Rodney Alcala was removed to San Quentin Penitentiary to await a date in the gas chamber.

The following month Alcala was taken from San Quentin to Riverside County Courthouse, where he stood trial for the rape of Monique Hoyt. The jury was overcome with emotion as they heard Monique's heartbreaking testimony. They were also sickened by photographs of Monique taken before and after her beating and rape. The stark and shocking contrast between her once happy and smiling and then bruised, beaten and crying face. Alcala had taken both sets of photographs himself. The jury found Alcala guilty, and the judge sentenced him to nine years imprisonment.

Alcala was appointed a new lawyer for the obligatory appeals process. On Sunday the 8th of February 1981, Keith Monroe appealed the murder conviction on several grounds. He said that the jail cell confession of the three inmates should have been ruled inadmissible as the inmates had been offered reductions in their sentences for their testimony. Monroe now had sworn testimony from one of the inmates, a man called John Mulqueen, stating that all three men had made up the confession initially to receive more favourable treatment in prison. Secondly, the judge should not have ruled Alcala's previous convictions admissible. Thirdly, during the jury selection stage of the trial, potential jury members had been removed by the prosecution as they had voiced opposition to the death penalty. Fourthly, the prosecution had told the jury that Robin had been sexually assaulted, yet the coroner had been unable to determine this fact. The initial appeal was rejected, but Monroe appealed this decision to the Californian Supreme Court.

On Thursday the 23rd of August 1984, the Californian Supreme Court overturned Alcala's conviction for the murder of Robin Samsoe on the grounds that his previous convictions had unduly biased the jury. The Samsoe family would have to face the daunting proposition of a retrial.

Rodney Alcala's second trial for the murder of Robin Samsoe took place in May 1986 before Judge Donald A. McCartin. The prosecution put forward the exact same evidence, minus the testimony of one of the three inmates who claimed Alcala had confessed to them and with no mention of Alcala's previous convictions. However, the prosecution added the written testimony of former U.S. Forestry Service Firefighter Dana Crappa, who had finally come to terms with discovering Robin's body. The defence now had witnesses who stated that Alcala had applied for a job as a photographer at Knott Berry Farm at around about the time Robin Samsoe had been murdered; however, under cross-examination, none of these witnesses could be 100% sure that this job interview had taken place on Saturday the 20th of June 1979. The defence also introduced phone records, which showed that several telephone calls had been made on the 20th of June 1979 at the home Alcala shared with his mother. These calls had been made to Elizabeth Kelleher. However, the prosecution took pains to point out that these records only showed that the calls were made, not who made them.

The jury went out to deliberate on Saturday the 24th of May 1986; they deliberated for four days. On Wednesday the 28th of May 1986, they returned with a unanimous guilty verdict. Once again, the jury was asked to consider the sentence. Before doing so, they were informed about Alcala's previous convictions, and in a masterstroke, the prosecution had tracked down Talia Shapiro, and she was brought into court to heartbreakingly tell the jury about what Rodney Alcala had done to her and how it had blighted her life. On Wednesday the 20th of August 1986, the jury returned to the courtroom to state that Alcala should face the death sentence. In response, Alcala had prepared a forty-nine-page deposition stating that his conviction was unsafe because his lawyers had been unprepared for the trial and had not provided an adequate defence. He requested that the conviction be dismissed. The motion was denied.

Rodney Alcala decided that he would act as his own defence lawyer in the future. He duly submitted his own handwritten appeal to the California Supreme Court. On Thursday the 31st of December 1992, the California Supreme Court upheld the conviction and death penalty. So, Alcala decided to try to win public sympathy. In 1994, he self-published a book entitled '*You, The Jury*' where he nit-picked at the circumstantial evidence and grumbled about minor inconsistencies in the prosecution's witness testimonies.

As time moved on, Alcala became quite the legal expert. He got a job in the prison law library and became a legal advisor to other inmates. As his legal knowledge grew, he sued the state of California twice, stating that his increasingly failing health and subsequent falls he had suffered were a result of the poor diet he received in prison. He also found time to appeal his second conviction to a higher Court. On Monday the 2nd of April 2001, the United States District Court for the Central District of California overturned Alcala's second conviction.

The second conviction was overturned on the grounds that Dana Crappa should have been summoned to the witness box so that the defence could cross-examine her. Over the years, Dana Crappa had proven to be quite the flaky witness, changing her story many times and making up different excuses for not reporting the discovery of Robin's body earlier. The District Court felt that the defence had a right to question Crappa about the inconsistencies in her many different versions of events. Robin's mother, Marianne Connelly, was inconsolable after the verdict, telling the press, *"We've been through a lot of hell because of that animal, a lot of hell."*

Alcala thought he was home and dry. Then, the state of California passed a new law that started to bring all his crimes home to roost. In 2002, California made it mandatory for all serving prisoners to submit a DNA sample so that it could be tested against any DNA evidence discovered in any unsolved crimes. If a prisoner refused, then reasonable force could be used to obtain the DNA sample. Alcala had no option but to comply with the law fully. Lo and behold, if Alcala's DNA didn't match that which had been left at the scenes of Jill Barcomb, Georgia Wixted, Charlotte Lamb and Jill Parenteau's murders.

With DNA linking Alcala to four more murders, the police investigating each crime began looking for more evidence against Alcala. Pretty soon, they gathered more and more damning evidence against Alcala, including positively identifying previously unidentified palm prints and bitemarks as belonging to Alcala, which had been found at the scene and on the victim's bodies. A Grand Jury was formed in Orange County to hear all the evidence against Alcala. The Grand Jury decided that Alcala was most likely responsible for each and every one of the crimes and gave the go-ahead for Alcala to be charged with all four murders.

On Tuesday the 7th of October 2003, Alcala appeared before Judge Fransico Pedro Briseno and formally pled not guilty for a third time to Robin Samsoe's murder. Alcala also informed the judge that he would act as his own defence attorney. A tentative trial date was set for early 2005. However, the trial was ultimately delayed due to the untimely death of one of the public defenders charged with helping Alcala mount his own defence.

On Saturday the 22nd of November 2003, Alcala appeared at the Orange County Superior Courthouse, where he stood accused of four murders, four rapes and torture. He pled not guilty. A further hearing was set for Friday the 13th of January 2006. The reason for the long delay was simple. Orange County District Attorney Tony Rackauckus hoped to get permission to amalgamate all five prosecutions into one trial. This would make an even stronger case against Alcala in all five cases and save public money by not having several separate trials in different county jurisdictions. However, to do so would mean establishing new case law and setting a precedent in cross-county prosecuting. The proceedings to try and make this common-sense approach a reality dragged on and became increasingly complicated and bogged down in legal wrangling.

On Wednesday the 28th of February 2007, the California Courts of Appeal decided that two trials would have to be held. One would deal with the murder of Robin Samsoe, Charlotte Lamb and Jill Parenteau, and the second would deal with Jill Barcomb and Georgia Wixted. The prosecution appealed this decision, and on Wednesday the 11th of June 2008, the California Supreme Court ruled that it made no sense to hold two separate trials and that all the cases should be tried together. The new trial judge then ruled that because of Alcala's lack of legal training and mental health diagnoses, he couldn't defend himself. Alcala appealed the decision. The 4th District Court of Appeal didn't get around to making a ruling on this decision until Monday the 14th of December 2009. They agreed that Rodney Alcala could defend himself at trial.

Finally, after almost nearly seven years of delays and legal upset Rodney Alcala's third and final trial commenced in earnest on Monday the 11th of January 2010. Alcala attended court casually dressed in a pair of jeans and a plaid shirt. He looked relaxed and confident that he would get an acquittal.

Initially, Alcala tried to be friendly with the prosecution lawyers. He had a 'call me Rod,' laid-back attitude. Deputy Prosecutor Matt Murphy was eager to disabuse Alcala of any notions that they were on friendly terms. He set out in the opening argument to destroy any credibility Alcala may have had with the jury and let Alcala know he would not be in for an easy ride, *"After my closing argument, That's when* (Alcala) *realised I was going to call him out and call him the devil. He realised I wasn't his friend."*

The prosecution's opening argument lasted an entire month. Deputy Prosecutor Matt Murphy has been described as "*a prosecutorial genius*" for his approach during the trial. Deputy Prosecutor Gina Santriano ably assisted. Together, they took the jury through a chronological blow-by-blow account of each crime, their similarities and how Rodney Alcala had been linked to each murder undeniably by DNA evidence.

During the testimony of the prosecution witnesses, Alcala asked very few questions when it came time for him to cross-examine. When he did, he mainly focused on nit-picking small and irrelevant points that didn't further his defence in any way whatsoever. The one point he tried to drum home to the jury was that no witness could be sure that on the day she disappeared, Robin Samsoe was wearing the earrings that were found in his lockup.

When it came time for the defence to make its case, the trial descended into one of the strangest proceedings in legal history. Like something out of a Marx Brothers film, Alcala cross-examined himself. He stood in the Courtroom and would ask a question in a slow, pompous and pondering voice. He would then run around the witness box, sit down, and answer the question in his normal avuncular tones. These bizarre antics dragged on for five hours, much to the bemusement of the jury.

The trial took a heartbreaking turn when Rodney Alcala asserted his right to cross-examine Marrianne Connelly. Alcala quizzed Marrianne intently over several hours about the earrings that Robin had been wearing on the day she died. Alcala wanted to establish that after thirty-one years, Marianne could not be certain Robin had been wearing the earrings at all. "*It was one of the* hardest things I've had to do in my life," Marianne would later emotionally say, "Having him ask me questions." The cross-examination infuriated everyone. Robin's sister, Taranne Mayes, was left distraught, "My heart was just ripped out because no person should be subjected to that." Matt Murphy explained in simple terms why he believed Alcala should never have been allowed to quiz Robin's mum, "This woman has had her credibility questioned... the third time around, Rod Alcala is representing himself, so she's getting cross-examined by the murderer of her daughter who's calling her a liar. Would you imagine that?" Gina Santriano agreed, "There are no words to describe how disturbing and uncomfortable and unfair that all felt." Detective Steve Mack, who had worked closely with Robin's family since the day Robin had disappeared, was still angry about the cross-examination even after the passage of several years and believed Alcala had an ulterior motive, "It got real frustrating for me that he was allowed to do that. Again, in my mind, he's reliving that incident through his questions of Robin's mother."

Alcala was entirely 100% focused on the murder of Robin Samsoe. It was as if he had entirely forgotten he was also on trial for murdering Charlotte Lamb, Jill Parenteau, Jill Barcomb and Georgia Wixted. He didn't bother to cross-examine witnesses in relation to these cases in any meaningful way. It seemed as if over the proceeding thirty years, he'd become completely obsessed with proving his innocence of Robin's murder and Robin's murder alone.

Alcala then took two hours to make a long, rambling and confused closing speech, which he seemed ill-prepared for and which he delivered in a dull, monotone voice. Alcala couldn't deny the damning DNA evidence that linked him to each crime, and his bizarre antics when cross-examining himself hardly endeared him to the jury. It seemed to everyone that he wasn't taking the proceedings seriously, and at times, he was having vicarious fun at the victim's expense. It took the jury just one hour to find Rodney Alcala guilty of murdering Robin Samsoe, Charlotte Lamb, Jill Parenteau, Jill Barcomb and Georgia Wixted. It was one of the quickest jury decisions in Orange County history.

Before deciding what sentence Alcala should face, the jury was first addressed by a court-appointed psychologist, Dr Richard Rappaport, who had carried out a detailed psychological assessment of Alcala. Dr Rappaport told the jury that Alcala suffered from a borderline malignant personality disorder categorised with psychopathy and sexual sadism co-morbidities. These conditions all hinged on abandonment issues linked to his father leaving the family when he was a child. Dr Rappaport stated that radical mood swings and psychotic episodes characterised these conditions. During such psychotic episodes, it was not uncommon for the sufferer to become detached from reality and to have no memory of their actions when the psychotic episode came to an end. It was, therefore, quite possible that Alcala could have been in a psychotic state when he committed his crimes and that he genuinely had no memory of committing the murders.

During the trial's penalty phase, Rodney Alcala continued his strange and antagonistic behaviours. CBS News Reporter Dave Lopez summed up Alcala's attitude during the penalty phase as "*Go ahead, give me the death penalty. I dare you. All it's going to do is lead to another appeal.*" Alcala asked the Court if he could play the jury a song before they decided his fate. Judge Briseno agreed to this strange request. In characteristic idiosyncratic style, Alcala had all 18 minutes and 34 seconds of Arlo Guthrie's 'Alice's Restaurant' played to the jury. It's an epic protest song about how a guy being arrested for flytipping endangers his eligibility for the military draft during the Vietnam War. There is a section of the song where Arlo Gutherie sings about his desire to kill, hurt people and see blood and gore, and angrily repeats the phrase 'kill' over and over again. Whilst allowing Alcala to play this song to the jury infuriated Matt Murphy, he realised that it ultimately sealed Alcala's fate, "*The jury understands the pain and the suffering reaped upon all of these families and all these people by Rodney Alcala, and he plays them a frigging song. I knew them; I knew they would be outraged by it, and I knew I had him in that moment.*"

On Tuesday the 9th of March 2010, the jury returned and informed the judge that they had decided that Rodney Alcala should face the death penalty. Alcala immediately put forward a motion to ignore the jury's decision, and he be sentenced to life imprisonment without the possibility of parole. Judge Briseno refused the motion and upheld the sentence of death.

Later that afternoon, the Orange County Prosecutor's office released to the press several hundred of the photographs found in Rodney Alcala's Seattle lockup. It was hoped that members of the public would recognise the women in the photographs and come forward.

In January 2011, a Grand Jury in New York arraigned Rodney Alcala for the murders of Cornelia Crilley and Ellen Jane Hover. In June 2012, Alcala was transferred from San Quentin Penitentiary to New York. He initially pleaded not guilty to the two murders. However, prosecutor Martha Bashford revealed that advanced forensic techniques had been able to recover one of Alcala's fingerprints from an envelope found in Cornelia Crilley's apartment. Not only this, DNA lifted from the bitemark in Cornelia's left breast had finally positively proved that he was her killer. Alcala decided not to waste anyone's time and changed his plea. On Monday the 7th of January 2013, Rodney Alcala received two concurrent life sentences for murdering Cornelia and Ellen, with a minimum of twenty-five years imprisonment to be served before he was eligible for parole.

Prosecutor Matt Murphy publically stated that he believed Alcala had many, many other victims, "*We always suspected there were more victims; we just didn't know who they were or could prove it.*" Slowly, other police forces across America also began to believe that Rodney Alcala was responsible for dozens of unsolved murders on their books.

In Wyoming, the police suspected Alcala of murdering a twenty-eight-year-old pregnant woman by the name of Ruth Thornton (known to her friends as Chris). She had disappeared in 1977 when she went gold hunting with her on/off boyfriend. Alcala became prime suspect when Ruth's sister identified an image of Ruth among the 1700 photographs found in Alcala's lockup. When Ruth was murdered, she was wearing the exact same clothes she was wearing in the photograph that Alcala had taken of her. Police interviewed Alcala about Ruth, and he admitted that he had known her and that, for a time, they had travelled together, but he denied killing her. Investigators didn't believe Alcala, and they got as far as charging Alcala with Ruth's murder, but by then, Alcala was an old man and had become too sick to travel to Wyoming to face trial.

In San Fransisco, police are convinced that Alcala murdered nineteen-year-old Pamela Lambson. Her beaten, battered and raped body was found near Mount Tamalpais. Before she disappeared, she told friends she was going to take part in a photoshoot with a man she met at Fisherman's Wharf in San Fransisco. Unfortunately, police were not able to recover DNA evidence in Pamel's case. Yet, the circumstances of her disappearance and death, along with the testimony of an eyewitness, leave them certain Alcala is the man responsible.

In New York, cold case investigator Detective Stefano Braccini believes Rodney Alcala is responsible for at least two other unsolved murders in the city. Braccini told the press, *"The witnesses describe Alcala to a T... It's him. It's definitely him."*

Other strange stories about Alcala abound. Victoria Best spent several years researching Rodney Alcala and trying to track down women who believed they'd been victims of Alcala's unreported and unprosecuted sex crimes. Best encountered a woman who she described as a credible witness related to a best-selling true crime author. This woman told Best that shortly before Alcala's arrest, she had been befriended by Alcala and persuaded by him to visit the house he shared with his mother. Alcala left the woman alone for a few moments, whereupon she went to find the bathroom. Instead, she found herself in a freezing cold bedroom, artificially cooled by an air conditioning unit. She claims that three seemingly drugged and beaten women were tied up in the bedroom. The witness was so scared she ran from the house and was too traumatised to reveal what she had seen to anyone for decades. It's an apocryphal story, like something out of a horror film, but it's said that the witness' veracity is beyond reproach.

Rodney Alcala never did see the inside of the gas chamber. He died of natural causes at Corcoran State Penitentiary near Fresno on Saturday the 24th of July 2021. He was seventy-seven. For many years, he'd been bedridden, left to stare at the peeling paint on the wall of his cell, suffering from a heart condition, Chronic Obstructive Pulmonary Disorder and dementia. Many were unhappy that Alcala hadn't seen the inside of the gas chamber, among them former police officer Chris Camacho, *"It wasn't justice because he died peacefully. Justice would have been if someone would have been choking him when he died... hopefully, he'll get justice in the next world because he certainly didn't get it here."*

As you read this book and think about the victims, not just those of Rodney Alcala, but the victims in every single case in this book, you are probably asking why. Why do these men murder women for their own demented pleasure? Forensic psychologist Rex Julian Beaber believes that in Rodney Alcala's case, there is no easy answer to these questions, *"Alcala appears to be a person who could have achieved many of his sexual desires without committing a homicide, and that makes him somewhat mystifying as serial killers go."*

But I think Rodney Alcala leads us to the best answer to all of the questions posed in this book. As Dr Elizabeth Yardley explained, "(Alcala is) *targeting prepubescent girls, he's targeting women, and sometimes he's taking pictures of young boys, but I think we shouldn't look at the differences between his victims. We need to look at what they've all got in common. They've all got in common a particular vulnerability, something that he sees as a weakness, something that he can prey on, so that's what he's looking for, and it doesn't really matter to him who he sees that in.*"

Essentially, every crime in this book is about weak and impotent men trying to disabuse themselves of their insecurities and assert their dominance over targets they can easily overcome, using physical power and control as a sickening aphrodisiac. Rodney Alcala ultimately helps to bring that brutal and disturbing fact into horrid focus.

Murder In Holy Orders: Sister Robin Elam

This was a violation, not just a violation of her, it was a violation of the church. – **Lieutenant Danny Swiger on the murder of Sister Robin Elam**

One of the most chilling crimes imaginable is the slaying and defiling of a holy person on holy ground. That is exactly what happened in our next case. A novice nun just days away from making her final commitment to God raped and murdered within the grounds of her holy retreat. It's a case that haunts those who investigate it. Indeed, Lieutenant Joe Cuchta went on record as saying that his only regret during his career as a law enforcement officer was that he failed to solve Sister Robin's murder. So let us pick up this fading Rubex Cube of a puzzle and make a few twists and turns of its pieces to see if we can find some semblance of truth.

Roberta Ann Elam was born on Wednesday the 23rd of August 1950, in Ramsey County, Minnesota, USA. The daughter of Robert Elam and Mary Rosella Elam nee Grogan. She was the eldest of four children and was described by her brother Chris as *"the leader of the pack."* Known as Robin to her friends, when Robin was still a child, the family moved to Wheaton, Illinois, where Robin attended St Francis High School. When you hear of someone training to become a nun, you imagine them having lived a religious and pious life since the day they were born. Saintly almost. It's good to hear, therefore, that Sister Robin was a normal teenager who dated and got into normal teenage hijinks. She played basketball and excelled at athletics. Young Robin had an interest in theology, and after graduating High School, she attended Fordham University in New York, where she read her favourite subject and ultimately graduated with a master's degree in theology.

Robin has been described by her family as "*progressive and outspoken*," and the police described her as "*outgoing, argumentative and personable.*" Chris Elam said of his sister, "*She was a rebel. She was one of these people who absolutely told everyone what she thought. Extremely direct. Very, very opinionated.*" She was, in every sense, what we would think of as a totally modern woman. Although Robin was training to be a nun, her ultimate aim was to try and shake up the catholic church from the inside and ultimately one day be ordained as a priest. Indeed, she told her family that she felt it was ludicrous that the catholic church placed such restrictions on women's rights. Chris Elam said of his sister, "*She was very none-nun-like.*" Indeed, what nun do you know drives around in an engine-roaring orange Fiat convertible Sportscar? She also had a deeply sensitive side and liked to write poetry, although some of it was a little morbid. Shortly before her untimely demise, Sister Robin wrote an intriguing poem about the nature of death.

Despite being outspoken and ahead of her time in many of her views and opinions, Sister Robin was trusted by the Diocese of Wheeling-Charleston, who appointed her as the coordinator of adult religious programs for the Diocese. This was a role that Sister Robin had undertaken for the twelve months prior to her death. Part of Sister Robin's job involved her venturing into the rural communities of West Virginia and trying to encourage the local residents to engage with the support services the Catholic Church offered.

In the days leading up to her death, Sister Robin was attending the Mount St Joseph's Retreat Centre, where she was to spend a few days in quiet reflection, deciding if she wanted to take her final vows and become a fully-fledged nun. Sister Robin had been directed to attend the retreat after disclosing to her spiritual advisor Sister Peggy Pairing that she was having doubts about taking holy orders. Sister Robin arrived at St Joesph's on Sunday the 5th of June 1977, and spent eight days carefully considering her future. The convent grounds bordered a public parkland, a residential estate and a golf course. The covenant's lands were not secured, and this meant that anyone could wander onto the grounds of the convent at any time they liked.

On Sunday the 12th of June 1977, Sister Robin went to speak with her best friend, Sister Kathleen Durkin. Sister Robin seemed out of sorts, a little distracted. Sister Kathleen asked Sister Robin what was on her mind, and Sister Robin replied that if she told Sister Kathleen about what was bothering her, then Sister Kathleen would probably think that Sister Robin was going out of her mind. Sister Kathleen assured Sister Robin that she would not, and that Sister Robin could tell her anything without judgement, but Sister Robin stubbornly refused to talk.

On Monday the 13th of June 1977, Sister Robin rose early and went for a jog around the covenant grounds. At 10.30 a.m., Sister Robin grabbed an apple from the convent's kitchen and went to meditate up on a hill a few hundred yards from the convent building. She sat on the bench in the morning sun and began pondering God's plan for her.

As Sister Robin sat quietly praying for holy guidance, an assailant crept up on her from behind. They grabbed Sir Robin in a choke hold and pulled her backwards, knocking over the bench. Once incapacitated, the murderous assailant carried Sister Robin forty feet downhill towards the treeline before placing her on the ground. This meant that they were out of the view of the golf course. The attacker then ripped down Sister Robin's jeans and knickers and pulled up her shirt and bra, exposing her breasts, before raping Sister Robin. The assailant then strangled Sister Robin to death using his bare hands. There were no defensive wounds on the body, and this led to the conclusion that Sister Robin was choked to unconsciousness as she sat on the bench. Sister Robin was a virgin and was on her period. She had a tampon inserted into her vagina, which the killer hadn't bothered to remove. At 1.50 p.m., a groundskeeper found Sister Robin's body, and he raised the alarm.

The Ohio County Sheriff's Office had jurisdiction over the case, and Detective Norm Sayre was placed in charge of the investigation. Sister Robin just so happened to be murdered at the same time that four other women had been raped and strangled in nearby Washington County. The Ohio County Sheriff's Office, therefore, had to investigate as a priority if Sister Robin's murder was related to the other four murders. On Wednesday the 15th of June 1977, Detective Norm Sayre met up with officers investigating the other murders, and after a long discussion, it was decided that Sister Robin's murder was unrelated to the other cases. The Washington State Killer used items of clothing to murder his victim. Sister Robin's killer used his bare hands. The Washington State Killer stripped his victims naked and scattered the clothes nearby. Sister Robin's clothes were left on the body. The killer's modus operandi was just too different for the cases to be connected.

One of the first actions was for the sheriff's department to contact the Speidel Golf Club and ask for a list of all the members who had been playing that Monday morning. All the golfers were investigated and questioned, and all were ruled out as suspects. Then the sheriffs turned their attention to workmen who had been removing telephone wires in the vicinity of the convent. They were tracked down to a salvage company based in Atlanta, Georgia. One of these men had a run-in with Sister Robin on the Friday before her murder. Sister Robin had overheard the workman making obscene remarks about the nuns. The promising lead ran aground when the workmen were tracked down, and all turned out to have cast-iron alibis.

Some of the staff at St Joseph's reported that the evening prior to the murder, there had been a man loitering in a black van. The van was spotted at approximately 10.30 p.m. outside the infirmary but was gone by 11.00 p.m. With no licence plate number or description of the driver, this wasn't very much for the sheriff's department to go on, and the potential lead fizzled out rather quickly. At around 11.00 a.m. on the day of the murder, some of the nuns in the building known as the mother house heard loud, high-pitched voices, but they assumed they belonged to golfers arguing on the nearby golf course. House-to-house enquiries carried out on a nearby housing estate uncovered no useful information. This frustrated the police as they believed the killer made his escape through the woods and down into this housing estate. The sheriffs had held hopes that one or more of the residents might have seen the murderer make their escape. No one had.

One person of interest was a man who had regularly been seen walking his dogs on the convent grounds in the months leading up to the murder. On the morning of the murder, he had been seen again on Pogue Run Road, just a few yards from the site where Sister Robin was murdered. The man was described as *"unkept, dark complexion, shaggy black hair, black eyes, and a beard, medium build, between 30 and 33 years old, and 5 feet 10 inches or 6 feet tall."* He was dressed in blue denim jeans and a blue denim jacket. He was also known to have a small brown poodle-like dog and to drive a faded blue or grey 1969 Chevrolet Impala that may have had West Virginian licence plates. The car was described by witnesses as being rusty and had some dents, and had three bumper stickers, two were said to be religious in nature, and one was related to coal mining. Witnesses also reported seeing several religious pamphlets in the back window of the vehicle.

The witness who saw the unkept man in his beaten-up car on the morning of the murder felt very uneasy about the man. There was something about him that hadn't sat right and lingered in their memory. Upon hearing of the murder later that day, the witness returned to Pogue Run Road to see if the car and its peculiar driver were still there. They were not. However, tyre marks on the road indicated that the car had driven off at high speed and had turned right at the intersection of Pogue Run Road and G C & P Road. If the suspect had continued along this road, it would have taken him to the Pennsylvanian border. An artist's impression of this possible suspect was drawn up by Special Investigator Richard Vulgamore, but the man never came forward to eliminate himself and was never traced.

On Thursday the 16th of June, Wheeling Police (who were not officially involved in the investigation) picked up a suspect in relation to an unrelated case. Intriguingly, Police Chief Edward Weith had an unidentified nun collected from Mount St Joseph's and transported to the Wheeling Police Head Quarters to view and possibly identify the suspect. When questioned about this development, Weith told reporters that the suspect was *"Just somebody we picked up on another case. We thought some connection could have been established."* It appears that this was just wishful thinking on the Wheeling Police's behalf, and the nun was promptly returned to the holy retreat.

A female Wheeling resident came forward to state that shortly before the murder, she had been flagged down near Mount St Joseph's Retreat Centre by a man who was wearing an Ohio Sheriff's Office uniform. When he approached the car, his manner was off, unnerving even, and the white gloves he was wearing smelt overpoweringly of chloroform. The woman became scared, and she drove off, leaving the dubious lawman at the side of the road. The Ohio Sheriff's Office investigated this possible lead, and like all others, it led nowhere.

With leads running dry and the incident room having received only 80 phone calls, the Sheriff's Office began to invite witnesses back in to be interviewed under hypnosis to see if this could elicit any further useful information. A public appeal was also made where Captain D. M. Shade requested that the citizens of Wheeling "wake up" and come forward with information. Captain Shade assured the public that they would not record or trace any calls they received, and if people wanted to write anonymously, they would not make any attempts to trace the letter writers. Indeed, the whole tone of the investigation was becoming exceedingly desperate.

Just as things were looking hopeless for the investigation, a promising suspect presented themselves. The suspect was a local man named John Jay Shoplak. An ex-military veteran, he was a violent man with a history of domestic violence, including a history of choking ex-partners. He also had a strong dislike of the catholic faith and anyone who practised it. He was described by his best friend as *"a weird and brutal person."* During one violent armed robbery where the victim was his own grandmother, Shoplak's rage boiled over when his grandmother could not remove a ring from her elderly finger, so he chopped his gran's finger off and took the ring *and* the finger. Shoplak had also previously been accused of raping two local girls. Shoplak came to the police's attention when he began to brag to friends that he had murdered a nun at St Joseph's. When the rumours reached the ears of the Sheriff's Office, Shoplak was arrested for Sister Robin's murder and was interviewed under caution. Indeed, Shoplak appeared to know details about the crime that had never been released to the public, such as Roberta having been ambushed from behind and her being a virgin who was on her period. However, Shoplak was exonerated of the murder when his blood type was found not to match that of the killers.

With the strongest suspect being ruled out as the killer and the case hitting dead end after dead end, the Federal Bureau of Investigation was brought in to assist. FBI Agent Tom Burgoyne said that when the FBI came to the investigation, *"Everyone involved with the investigation was pretty frustrated at this point because everyone believed it should have been an open-and-shut case."* Burgoyne felt that the case had been mishandled from the get-go, and he felt that this was due to the fact that those investigating the crime were not highly trained law enforcement officers with years of experience but elected officials. Burgoyne went on record as saying, *"If you talked to anyone who was involved with the case from the very beginning, they will tell you that it was mishandled pretty badly... In 1977, when the voters elected a new sheriff, he brought his own people in for the deputy positions, and that meant a guy could have been a farmer one day and a sheriff's deputy the next day."*

Like the Sheriff's Office, FBI Agents can only be as good as the leads they are given. Sister Robin's murder appeared to be entirely random, with no other motive other than sex. The FBI found themselves as lost as the local law enforcement officers, and the case progressed not one iota. It fell stale and stagnant, and there was no further progress for forty-two years.

In 2019, as part of a cold case review, Sister Robin's diary was given to forensic psychologist Dr Judy Ho. Dr Ho concluded that Sister Robin was a very conflicted person, struggling not just with her commitment to God but with her self-esteem. Whilst the diary discussed Sister Robin's struggles with her faith, it did not discuss her day-to-day activities. It was *"very abstract for a diary."* Dr Ho concluded that the diary was incomplete. It seemed as if Sister Robin was holding things back, perhaps believing that someone was secretly reading her diary and scared that her secrets would come out, she was therefore compartmentalising it. Dr Ho postulated that Sister Robin may have had a secret diary where she discussed her day-to-day life, her interactions and her secret innermost thoughts. If there was a second diary, it has never been recovered.

When several of the surviving nuns from St Joseph's were asked by the cold case review team if they had any idea about who might have been responsible for Sister Robin's murder, one of the nuns replied, "*The most suspicious pool of people were the priests.*" So, as a matter of priority as part of a cold case review of the murder, all of the priests who had been working at St Joseph's at the time of the murder submitted DNA samples for analysis. None were a match for the killer's DNA. The priests might have acted suspiciously, but they weren't murderers.

The cold case review focused once again on John Jay Shoplak. It was discovered that the police had uncovered Shoplak's blood type not through blood testing but by consulting his military records. It was now known that many military records from the mid-twentieth century were wholly unreliable and often stated erroneous medical information due to the cheap and often faulty methods used to ascertain the blood type. It also didn't take into account people with the rare genetic condition chimerism who have two blood types. Due to this, it was hoped that a sample of Shoplak's DNA could be acquired so that it could be compared to that of the killers. Unfortunately, Shoplak died in August 2019, and his family refused the Ohio State Sheriff's Office's request for a DNA sample.

The killer's DNA is now in the Combined DNA Index System. Whenever a criminal new to the Criminal Justice System has their DNA taken, it will be fed into CODIS, and it will automatically be compared to the DNA of Sister Robin's killer. The DNA left behind by the fiend has already allowed 20 suspects to be ruled out. Detective Doug Earnest, who is currently in charge of the cold case investigation, has gone on record as saying that the last best hope of Sister Robin's killer being brought to justice is by his DNA, "*I really believe that if this case gets solved, it will be from the DNA,*" Detective Earnest said, before adding a sobering coda, "*Unless this person was pretty young when he committed these crimes, he is probably pretty old right now if not dead already.*"

The Deadliest Swinger In Town: Selena Anne Keough, Mary Susan Duggan and Janna Rowe

"You'd have to believe this defendant is the most unlucky person on the planet to have three women all turn up dead with the defendant's semen inside them" - **Los Angeles County Deputy District Attorney Beth Silverman on Horace Van Vaultz.**

Sometimes, it just takes time for a killer to get their just deserts. It can seem like a case is unsolvable, that all hope is lost, and that even the police have given up. But, with the relentless march of technological progress, no killer is safe from justice. This next case highlights how time, perseverance and the latest advances in forensic policing can catch a killer when all hope of answers and justice is seemingly lost.

Selena Anne Keough was born on Monday the 26th of October 1959, to Arthur and Thelma Keough. She was a doting single mother. Yet, despite her responsibilities, she was still young, and like most people her age, Selena liked to go out dancing. On the evening of Wednesday the 15th of July 1981, Selena went to Club Unicorn on Holt Boulevard, Montclair, California. The club wasn't far from Selena's apartment, so after the night of dancing and enjoying herself, she decided to walk home. The next morning, her body was found stripped naked and tied up under a bush near her apartment. Selena had been anally raped and strangled. There was nothing for the police to go on. Selena had no enemies in the world. They could find no one who would want to do her harm. She had a good relationship with the father of her child, and he had a cast iron alibi for the night of the murder. There were no eyewitnesses or anyone who saw anything strange or untoward in the nightclub. The investigation petered out and the case became another infuriatingly unsolved mystery.

Mary Susan Duggan was born on Sunday the 3rd of May 1964. Just like Selena Keough, Mary loved to party and regularly hung around local nightclubs and discotheques. She was last seen in a bar on Vanowen Street in the Reseda district of Los Angeles. A little after midnight on Tuesday the 10th of June 1986, Mary's body was found hidden under some newspapers in the boot of her 1980 Ford Mustang, which had been parked at a carpark on the intersection of Glenoaks Boulevard and Cohasset Street. Mary was naked and tied up. She had been raped and had choked to death on a tissue that had been rammed with some force down her throat. The autopsy indicated that she had been intercepted whilst on her night out, as it revealed that there was a moderate amount of cocaine and alcohol in Mary's system.

Detective Craig Ratliffe was placed in charge of the investigation. However, just like in the case of Selena Keough, he quickly found the case to be an investigative blackhole. By Saturday the 28th of June 1986, Ratliffe admitted to the Los Angeles Times he had no leads to follow and no viable suspects.

Janna Rowe was born on Wednesday the 23rd of October 1963 in Salt Lake City, Utah. Like the previous two victims, she was a frequent visitor to local nightclubs where she loved to dance and enjoy the music. On Saturday the 27th of December 1986, her body was found dumped on a rubbish tip in Thousand Oaks, California. She was naked and had been tied up and raped orally, vaginally and anally. Police carried out enquiries in the local neighbourhood and discovered several witnesses who had seen Janna going into a room at a local motel. The room had been rented by a thirty-one-year-old known sex offender by the name of Horace Van Vaultz Jr.

Vaultz was divorced and lived an itinerant lifestyle, travelling all over California, Texas and Missouri, not stopping in one place for long before moving on. He also liked using different names and had a string of aliases, including Dianne Trevino, Horace Van and Devlin Vaultz. Not only did he involve himself in petty crimes, but there had also been a string of sexual assault allegations that had followed him around, and in 1984, he was arrested and pleaded no contest to a sexual assault and sexual choking allegation. When not in trouble with the law, he sometimes described himself as working in the music industry and was known to hang around nightclubs pretending to be a DJ or music executive so that he could lure vulnerable drunk women into dangerous situations.

Police ultimately tracked Vaultz to his mother's address, and they carried out a search of the property. During this search, they discovered his mother's jewellery box had some of Janna's jewellery hidden inside. Vaultz found himself being charged with Janna's murder.

The case against Vaultz was purely circumstantial. There was no smoking gun. It was long before DNA could put beyond reasonable doubt someone's guilt. Vaultz admitted that he knew Janna. He admitted that he had spent time with her in the motel room. He admitted that he had stolen some of her jewellery. He vehemently denied killing her. Being a seedy lothario and thief was far, far from being a murderer. The defence was able to put enough reasonable doubt into the jury's mind, and they acquitted Vaultz of Janna's murder.

In 2020, Sergeant Aaron Kay was tasked with re-examining some of Los Angeles' cold cases, "*When you have cold cases, you're always looking for new ways to solve them and asking, 'Is that a method we can use in our case?'.*" Kay would later tell the press. He decided that to try and crack the seemingly unsolvable cases, he would use a method that had been utilised during the cold case investigation of the Golden State Killer, which ultimately led to the arrest and conviction of Joseph DeAngelo. Kay secured a Court Order that instructed a genealogical website to hand over their DNA database. Over many years, people had sent the company samples of DNA to try and trace distant relatives and learn more about their family's genetic heritage. Using the private company's DNA database and with the help of the FBI's Forensic Genetic Genealogy Team, Kay was able to find familial DNA that closely matched that which had been left behind by the killer of Selena Keough, Janna Rowe and Mary Duggan. Putting it simply, this private database allowed the police to identify relatives of the killer (cousins or siblings), and from this, they could then zero in on the killer himself. Lo and behold, Horace Van Vaultz Jr was again the prime suspect.

Police obtained another warrant that allowed them to search through Vaultz's rubbish bins. They recovered items with Vaultz DNA on them and sent them for testing. These DNA tests proved that it had been Holtz's semen inside the corpses of Selena Anne Keough, Mary Susan Duggan and Janna Rowe.

In the thirty-seven years since standing trial for Jenna's murder, Vaultz had continued to constantly move around. He'd entered into a string of volatile relationships and been charged several times with domestic battery. In 1996, he'd taken a plea deal to avoid prison time after beating his partner senseless. He had no real roots but managed to elicit sympathy by describing himself as a widow.

On the morning of Thursday, the 14th of November 2019, Vaultz was stopped by police whilst driving his car near his home in Inglewood, California, and arrested for the murder of Selena and Mary. Unfortunately, due to the double jeopardy laws, Vaultz could not be charged with Janna's murder even though the police had incontrovertible proof that he was her killer. Shortly afterwards, a search of Vaultz's home address was carried out, and in a situation that was eerily similar to Rodney Alcala, police found hundreds of photographs of women. This left Sergeant Kay wondering if these women could be more victims of Vaultz.

Vaultz denied everything, of course. Within three days of his arrest, Vaultz's lawyer, Damon Lamont Hobdy, told the press, *"Their contention is that it's a DNA case. DNA can be faulty."*

Horace Van Vaultz Jr.'s trial for the murder of Selena Anne Keough and Mary Susan Duggan began at Los Angeles County Superior Court on Wednesday the 6th of July 2022, before Judge Ronald S. Coen. It was the first cold case trial in LA County history to make use of genealogical data. Although Vaultz had been acquitted of the murder of Janna Rowe, the prosecution was allowed to use her murder as evidence of Vaultz's pattern of violence against women.

Hobdy put forward what became known as *"the swinger's defence."* Hobdy stated that Vaultz had cheated on his wives and girlfriends and was *"not perfect,"* but this didn't mean he was a serial killer. Expanding on the defence, he told the jury, *"It is reasonable to conclude that sex happened, and sometime later, these women were killed. Yeah, the DNA is pretty strong. But DNA doesn't cry out to you and say, 'Oh, this, by the way, is the person who committed this crime'."*

Vaultz even took to the stand in his own defence and explained that in the 1980s, he had been a swinger and had hundreds of sexual partners. As a result, he couldn't remember specifically having sex with the three victims but conceded he must have done so. Crucially, he testified that he had not murdered them. Beth Silverman pooh-poohed this idea and asked the jury to consider what the odds would be of Vaultz having sex with three women who were then all killed within a few hours whilst his semen was still in their vaginas. Straining belief even further, what were the odds of the bodies then being dumped close to where Vaultz lived and worked?

Summing up the prosecution's case, Beth Silverman told the jury, "*The defendant left a horrific trail behind him of naked, broken, bruised, dead bodies behind. But he also left behind his unique fingerprint, and that is his genetic profile.*" Damon Lamont Hobdy countered the prosecution with a much weaker closing argument, telling the jury, "*If the evidence shows he's not guilty, which it does, do your duty.*"

The jury deliberated for three hours before returning with a guilty verdict. Vaultz was sentenced to two consecutive life sentences without the possibility of parole. After the sentencing, Beth Silverman said it was "a *great moment to see the end of this reign of terror.*" Damon Lamont Hobdy got as close to admitting that he had never believed in his client's innocence as a lawyer can when he told the press, "*I think Mr Vaultz got a fair trial.*"

After the trial, the victim's families addressed the press. Selena's sister, Sabrina Plourde, told reporters, "*I'm feeling incredibly grateful for everybody that helped us get to this point. You think for so many years nobody cares. ... They do care, and they won't forget, and they won't forget about the family if you're missing someone.*" Maureen Duggan, Mary Duggan's mother, lamented, "*It's one thing that your child dies at only twenty-two years old. It's a whole other thing to know she suffered in dying at the hands of a monster.*" Marcia Conner, the mother of Janna Rowe, said, "*I've had to live with the knowledge that we would never find justice*" and admitted that the guilty verdict was "*bittersweet.*" Janna's brother, Jeffery, added, "*Horace Van Vaultz Jr., oh, how I loathe that name. It makes me ill just to speak it. I've despised the defendant since he was acquitted of murdering my sister Janna in 1988, knowing full well in my mind he was guilty. How unjust to have him alive and free on the same Earth as us for the last thirty-seven years... I'm actually sad that he is not being sentenced to death. That seems the only tolerable sentence for people as evil as the defendant."*

Horace Van Vaultz preyed upon the vulnerabilities of young women. He sought his victims out at some of their weakest moments when they were drunk and had their guards down. Yet, this pattern of violent and vile behaviour throughout his adult life shows not only what a predator he was but how pathetic and insecure he was when in a normal adult relationship. So pathetic he regularly had to resort to violence to assert his dominance over his partners and make himself feel good, more of a 'man.' Horace Van Vaultz is the epitome of toxic masculinity, a man obsessed with sex but emotionally ill-equipped to deal with any adult feelings that come with it. I wonder how many more victims he had, ones he not only raped, beat and sexually assaulted but murdered, for a man like Horace Van Vaultz is hardly likely to have stopped at just three.

The Beauty In The Bath: Cynthia Bolshaw

In twenty-four years in the CID, I have never come across a more intriguing case. Agatha Christie could have written it – **Detective Superintendent Jim Owens.**

The little township of Heswall on the idyllic Wirral Peninsula is a quiet place. Known as one of the most affluent areas in the whole of the UK, it at one time ranked as the 7th richest neighbourhood in the whole country. It's been home to celebrities, sports personalities, rock musicians, and no less than two spouses of former Prime Ministers. It was in this exclusive little neighbourhood that our next murder took place.

Cynthia Rosemary Bolshaw was born in Liverpool in 1933, the youngest of four children born to Elsie and Charles Wilson. When Cynthia was still an infant, the family moved to West Kirby on the Wirral Peninsula, where Charles Wilson opened a bookshop. In April 1956, Cynthia married Captain James Ferrington Bolshaw, who came from the nearby village of Greasby. James was a pilot in the Royal Air Force. In July 1957, the couple had a son whom they called Christopher. However, the pair were an ill-suited couple, and the marriage lasted just seven years, the couple divorcing in 1963. Nevertheless, Captain Bolshaw continued to provide for his son, and he paid for Christopher to attend Birkenhead School, a rather exclusive private educational facility in Oxton village on the Wirral.

By 1983, Cynthia was fifty years old and had never remarried. Christopher Bolshaw had very recently married and moved to Yorkshire. Cynthia now lived with only her pet cat Gomez for company in a luxury bungalow on Buffs Lane, Heswall. Cynthia was a new resident of the exclusive little neighbourhood, having moved to Heswall in March 1983. She had, for the previous fifteen years, lived in the picturesque chocolate box village of Burton. Here she had been a well-known figure in the local community. Cynthia had many friends in the village. Cynthia's friends and neighbours were a little baffled by Cynthia's decision to move from the idyllic little picture-book village that overlooked the Burton Marshes. Indeed, curiously, Cynthia refused to explain to people whom she had been friends with for so many years her sudden decision to move. We do know that Cynthia may have regretted the move to Heswall, for she was certainly looking to move again.

Cynthia was a very attractive woman and was no wilting violet. She kept a daily diary and contained in these seventeen books, which spanned a fifteen-year period of her life, were the salacious details of the sexual exploits she'd had with over three hundred men. Indeed, it was this one detail that made the case a tabloid sensation back in 1983. Of course, Cynthia knew how to be discreet. The gentlemen she enjoyed the company of were not named. They were given coded nicknames. The oil-rig worker, the carpet fitter, the estate agent, the magician, the ex-marine, the farmer, the solicitor, the Ugandan police officer, the captain in the Sultan of Oman's army.

Cynthia's diaries highlighted just what a modern woman Cynthia was. Cynthia was an outgoing woman who made sure she got what she wanted in life. She scandalised her prudish neighbours by sunbathing in the back garden wearing nothing but a G-string. When out for a meal one evening, she seduced the owner of the restaurant, had him close up early, and had sex with him on the floor of the restaurant. When having a gentleman caller around one evening, a second gentleman friend called around unexpectedly. Cynthia persuaded both men to share her favours that evening. She seduced a member of the Cheshire Serious Fraud Squad and, as a lasting memento, gave him a picture of herself lying naked on a fur rug.

As an added bonus to her many love affairs, Cynthia's suitors would often buy her expensive gifts. One married veterinarian who lived in Chester bought her a little sports car. A customs officer took her on an all-expenses paid trip to Dubai. There was one suitor who, it appears, was even planning on buying Cynthia a property in Chester. Cynthia and the unidentified lover had contacted Beresford and Adams Estate Agents in Chester and made arrangements to visit any bungalows that came on the market in the Chester area. Other lovers would simply take Cynthia for expensive meals at fancy restaurants, where Cynthia would take great joy in eating the most expensive meal on the menu and drinking champagne and expensive wines.

Despite living in an exclusive neighbourhood in a property few of us could ever hope to afford, Cynthia lived a financially precarious life. In a neighbourhood of millionaires, Cynthia had savings of less than £40,000. To keep up appearances, she juggled various jobs, such as being a barmaid, a hotel receptionist and most latterly, a salesperson on the Dior counter at the exclusive Browns of Chester department store[vii]. Cynthia's friend, Valerie Johnson Hamer, said that as Cynthia grew older, she increasingly regretted not settling down with just one stable partner. Indeed, Cynthia was becoming increasingly depressed by her circumstances.   Shortly prior to her murder, Cynthia disclosed to a colleague that one suitor, in particular, was becoming a nuisance.   This man kept calling at Cynthia's bungalow in the early hours of the morning or late in the evening, and all he wanted was sex.   Cynthia stated that this man left her feeling like "*a public convenience.*"

The weeks leading up to Cynthia's murder had been a busy time for Cynthia. Cynthia was enjoying living by herself again.   After graduating from Manchester University, Christopher and his fiancé Gaynor moved back in with Cynthia whilst they saved up for a deposit on a house of their own.   On Saturday the 1st of October 1983, Cynthia had the joy of watching her son marry.   After exchanging vows at Barnton Parish Church, Christopher and Gaynor spent one last night at the bungalow in Buffs Lane before moving to Yorkshire.   It was arranged for Cynthia, her sister and her brother-in-law to visit Chris and Gaynor in their new home on Sunday the 9th of October 1983.

On the evening of Saturday the 8th of October 1983, Cynthia arrived home from work at 6.20 p.m.   At 11.30 p.m., Mrs Elliott, one of Cynthia's neighbours, was out walking her dog past Cynthia's house. They noted that the porch light of Cynthia's bungalow was on, a light Cynthia usually left on when she was expecting male company.   Importantly, Cynthia's red Toyota Corolla was also still parked on the driveway.

On the morning of Sunday the 9th of October 1983, Cynthia's sister and brother-in-law arrived at the bungalow in Buff's Lane at 10.30 a.m. as arranged to collect Cynthia.   Intending to make the journey to visit Christopher and

Gaynor in Yorkshire. Cynthia, however, did not come out of the bungalow, and her car was missing from the driveway. Cynthia's sister got out of the car and went to knock on the front door. She got no reply. So, she moved around to the back of the house and found that the back door was open. Cynthia's sister entered the house and found Cynthia lying face down in the bath in approximately 18 inches of water. Cynthia was naked apart from earrings, a necklace and a gold bangle. She was covered in small bruises and had been strangled, and had also received a blow to the side of her head. On Cynthia's bed lay a black negligee with semen stains upon it. The bungalow had not been ransacked, but jewellery was missing. Cynthia's Toyota Corolla car was also missing. Later that day, the car was found abandoned at the entrance to a field eight miles away off the A540 Chester High Road.

The investigation into Cynthia Bolshaw's murder was a nightmare from the start and difficult to solve because of one mistake made by an inexperienced police officer. This young officer was one of the first officers on the scene, and he stupidly let the water out of the bath, intending to give Cynthia CPR. When the young police officer realised what he had done and that he had probably destroyed valuable forensic evidence, he tried to cover his tracks by filling the bath up again with hot water. This altered Cynthia's body temperature and made it almost impossible to say with any certainty what time she died. The two pathologists who conducted autopsies on the body gave times of death as varied as 3.00 a.m., 4.00 a.m. and even 6.00 a.m. on the morning of Sunday the 9th of October 1983. In stark contrast, a local GP who was called to the crime scene and who examined Cynthia in situ at 11.15 a.m.

noted that the bath water was still warm and believed that Cynthia had been dead less than an hour or two.

Police pieced together Cynthia's last moments. They believed the murder had taken place in the bedroom. Where Cynthia was beaten and strangled as she lay on the bed. The police deduced this from the urine-soaked sheets. The killer then went to the bathroom, where he ran a bath before dumping Cynthia's naked body face down into the water. The killer then searched for Cynthia's jewellery and stole it. There was no sign of forced entry into the bungalow, and alongside the back door being unlocked, the window of Cynthia's bedroom had been left wide open. Strangely, the door to the fridge had also been left open as if Cynthia had been disturbed whilst getting something from the fridge.

There were blood spots on the bedsheets, on a doorjamb, and there were bloodied kitchen towels in the kitchen. Police believed Cynthia had cut her finger on a broken glass on the evening of her murder, and these towels were the result of her trying to stem the flow of blood. Brown fibres from a pair of corduroy trousers were found on the bedsheets, bedroom stool, Cynthia's negligee and on the driver's seat of Cynthia's car. On the bedsheets, there was also traces of a reddish-brown shoe polish and small particles of grey stone. There was a fingerprint on the inside of the bedroom window frame that the police were never able to identify. The police also discovered those diaries that made the case such an instant tabloid sensation. Tellingly, out of the seventeen diaries, only one single page was missing. Torn hastily from one of the more recent books.

Head of Birkenhead Criminal Investigation Department Detective Superintendent Jim Owens was placed in charge of the investigation, and he set up an enquiry room at Bebington Police Station. He told the reporters at a press conference, "*Death was due to asphyxia, she certainly did not drown, and we are not looking for a weapon.*" Pretty soon, the investigation became one of the biggest murder investigations in Merseyside Police's history. Eighty-four police officers were assigned to the case. A number of police officers were labelled the 'The Boyfriend Squad' and were tasked with trawling through Cynthia's diaries looking for clues. All in all, 290 house-to-house enquiries were conducted, and 4000 phone calls were logged in the incident room. The police took 1500 statements and spoke to 64 men under police caution. The Boyfriend Squad ultimately tracked down 200 of Cynthia's gentlemen friends and was able to clear them of any wrongdoing. Yet over 100 men remained untraced and unaccounted for.

In an unprecedented move, the villagers of the village of Ness, five miles south of Heswall, opened their homes to the police and allowed their properties to be searched without warrant. Five hundred properties in Ness were painstakingly searched by the police, yet it yielded no results. The police never revealed why the village of Ness became so central to the enquiry for such a short period. Some believe that this may have been the result of a series of hoax calls that the incident room received. These telephone calls ultimately led to thirty-seven-year-old Gloria Holmes from Salford, Greater Manchester, being prosecuted for wasting over 100 hundred hours of police time. Holmes said she gave the police false information because she was "*bored and lonely.*"

Holmes ultimately received a two-year Probation Order with the condition that she had to take part in psychiatric treatment.

Interpol was contacted and asked to make enquiries with foreign police forces in France, Germany, Italy, the United Arab Emirates, Japan, the United States of America and Uganda to try and track down as many of the men alluded to in Cynthia's diaries as possible. Local taxi firms were contacted to see if anyone and been dropped off or collected from Buffs Lane on the Saturday evening or early hours of the Sunday morning. No one had.

Eventually, a photofit was released of a person of interest. A thin-lipped man in his mid-fifties wearing spectacles. He was described as being short and stocky, broad-shouldered, with a round face and clean-shaven and with short grey receding hair and wearing silver frame glasses. It was later revealed that this person of interest was the man who had been seen with Cynthia enquiring about bungalows for sale in the Chester area.

The house-to-house enquiries yield some results. A neighbour of Cynthia's stated that in the early hour of Sunday the 9th of October, they almost ran over a male of heavy build with shoulder-length hair who ran out into the road coming from the direction of Cynthia's bungalow. A second neighbour informed the police that Cynthia had disclosed that someone had been stealing her underwear from her washing line, and she had received a series of anonymous sexually explicit and heavy-breathing style phone calls.

Interviewing the staff at Browns of Chester brought to the police's attention another possible suspect. This unlikely killer was an elderly customer who had an *"uncomfortable obsession"* with Cynthia. This man was said to be in his sixties with white hair, five-foot-seven to five-foot-eight in height, of medium build with an oval face and usually wore an anorak or green nylon parker-style jacket. He also usually carried a shoulder bag and wore a hearing aid. This suspect would come into Browns of Chester every Friday and simply stand at a distance staring at Cynthia. When challenged by staff, the man revealed that he clearly suffered from a speech impediment.

A highly credible witness, who was familiar with Cynthia, approached the police and provided a statement. According to this witness, on Tuesday the 4th of October 1983, at 7.30 p.m., they personally observed Cynthia standing next to her car at the entrance to a field off the A540 Chester High Road. This location would later become the site where Cynthia's killer ultimately abandoned her vehicle. Cynthia's car was parked next to a Y registration metallic bronze Mercedes Benz S-Class saloon. The driver of the Mercedes was a well-built, six-foot-tall, forty- to fifty-year-old male with short dark hair. Was Cynthia meeting this man at this location just a peculiar and chilling coincidence, or was this possibly a sighting of Cynthia with her killer?

A witness called Mr Dawson came forward to state that he remembered seeing Cynthia's car parked on the Chester High Road at 4.30 a.m. on the morning of Sunday the 9th of October. There was a man standing beside the car. He was in his mid-fifties with dark, curly hair, glasses and wearing a long Crombie overcoat. This was extraordinarily similar to the description of the man who had been enquiring about bungalows with Cynthia in Chester in the weeks leading up to her murder.

At around 4.50 p.m. on Tuesday the 11th of October 1983, fifty-two miles from Heswall, in the village of Romiley, a member of the public entered a phone box and noticed a nylon stocking seemingly abandoned on the floor. The stocking had been made into a rudimentary facemask, and inside was all of the jewellery stolen from Cynthia's bungalow. The items in the stocking were an engagement ring valued at £2,500, a gold wedding ring, and a designer wristwatch. The stocking did not match any belonging to Cynthia. The stocking contained fibres from Cynthia's bedspread and traces of the brown corduroy fibres found at the scene of the murder and in Cynthia's car. This, therefore, proved one very important point. The stocking mask did not originate from the scene of the murder but must have been present in the bedroom when Cynthia was murdered. As it had been present at the scene of the murder, we can say with great certainty that the stocking mask wasn't a hastily conceived red herring made in the days after the murder and used by the killer to try and throw the police off the scent.

Despite the plethora of information that the police had received from a public eager to help, the case cooled. There was the occasional bid to relight the public's imagination, a £3000 reward in 1990, and a reconstruction on Crimewatch. In 1992, two serving prisoners were interviewed about Cynthia's murder. The prisoners were male and female. During the course of her interview, the female prisoner confessed to giving her former partner a false alibi for the night of Cynthia's murder. Despite this new information, the case remained stubbornly unsolvable.

It took fifteen years for an arrest to be made. They say you should fear the wrath of a woman scorned. Well, Barbara Cragg felt deeply aggrieved with her ex-husband John Edwin Taft, and she no longer wished to keep to herself that he had asked her to lie to the police about his whereabouts on the night of Cynthia's murder. Barbara told a friend about Taft's request for a false alibi, and the friend dutifully went to the police and passed the information along. John Taft had been interviewed by the police back in 1983, as the police had found his business card and a business letter from his company amongst Cynthia's belongings. Taft lied and told the police that Cynthia had been nothing more than a customer he'd met once to give a quote to, and he wasn't even sure if he'd have recognised her if he'd met her again. John Taft had, in fact, been one of Cynthia's many lovers. They had first met when Taft went to give Cynthia a quote for double-glazing. During the consultation, Cynthia seduced Taft, and they became regular lovers.

Police used DNA profiling which had not been available back in 1983, to test the semen stains found on the black negligee at the scene of the murder. The DNA results came back as a 100% match for John Taft. On Thursday the 15th of April 1999, he found himself being arrested and charged with Cynthia's murder.

John Taft was a forty-nine-year-old successful local businessman. The director of a double-glazing company. He had been raised in Birkenhead. He'd had a difficult childhood; both his parents were alcoholics. Despite this, John had done well for himself, and at the time of the murder, he lived in a large property on Mostyn Avenue, which was just a short five-minute drive from Cynthia's bungalow. He'd met his first wife, Barbara Cragg, via a dating magazine, and the couple had married just six months after first meeting. Taft was well embedded in the Heswall community and was a member of a local amateur dramatics group called the Woolgatherers. He had no criminal convictions on his antecedent history, and just nineteen days before his arrest, he had married his second wife, Susan Hogan.

John Taft's trial commenced at Liverpool Crown Court on Wednesday the 10th of November 1999, before Judge David Clarke. Clarke was a man who had been raised on the Wirral. He'd attended the exclusive Winchester College, a prestigious public school in Hampshire, before reading law at Magdalen College, Oxford. He was called to the bar in 1965, working as a jobbing barrister on the northern circuit. He was appointed Queen's Council the very same year Cynthia Bolshaw was murdered. In 1992 he was awarded a judgeship, and many saw this as a just reward for his excellent work as leading counsel to the Sir John May Enquiry into the Guilford Four and Woolwich Bombings.

In 1997 Clarke was promoted to the role of Honorary Recorder of Liverpool[viii] and the Senior Circuit Judge for the Northern Circuit. During this time, Judge Clarke drew praise for his innovative work whilst chairman of the Criminal Justice Strategy Committee, which was instrumental in bringing closer links between the Police, CPS, Probation and Prison Service at a time when most of these organisations weren't on speaking terms.

In 2003, Judge Clarke was appointed by the Queen to the High Court, Queens Bench Division, where he was given the customary knighthood. He took on the role of Presiding Judge for the Northern Circuit, which effectively meant he was the senior line manager of all the judges sitting in the north of England. He was held in great affection by the other judges, who nicknamed him '*The Headmaster*,' and his style as a judge was described as "*unpretentious, sincere and compassionate.*"

Despite much of his work in the high court increasingly forcing him to spend time in London, Clarke continued to live on the Wirral peninsular. An avid supporter of the Wirral-based Tranmere Rovers Football Club, he was also a regular attendee at Oxton Cricket Club.

Oliver Blunt QC for the defence has been described as "*one of the longstanding leaders of the bar,*" others have said he is "*a master tactician with an absolute command of the courts,*" he's been "*universally acclaimed,*" and others have said he's "*a first-class silk for heavyweight criminal trials such as murder.*" He does it all with "*panache and drama*" and holds "*enviable cross-examination skills*" and "*a frighteningly clever magnetic presence in the courtroom.*" Over the years, he's defended a right rogues gallery of murderers, terrorists, and gangsters. Serial killers Peter Tobin and Michael Sams, DJ-rapist Richard Baker, blackmailing police officer Amerdeep Johal, and Millennium Dome robber William Cockram have all availed themselves of Blunt's services. To this day, Blunt regularly appears on the annual list of highest-earning barristers.

The prosecution was led by Andrew Edis QC. Like Judge Clarke, Edis was a local man having been brought up and educated in Liverpool. He read law at University College Oxford before returning to his home city, where he was called to the bar in 1980. He slowly gained a reputation as one of the top criminal advocates in the country. In 1994 he was made Assistant Recorder of Liverpool. In 2001 he was appointed Deputy High Court Judge and was made a Senior Treasury Council member in 2008. Over the course of his career, he had conducted many high-profile prosecutions, from the 'Lady In The Lake' murder case to prosecuting Chris Huhne, the Secretary of State for Energy and Climate Change, when he attempted to pervert the course of justice. Edis was also the lead counsel in the prosecution of the News of the World editorial staff in the aftermath of the phone hacking scandal that led to that newspaper's demise.

Andrew Edis QC was assisted by a junior barrister called David Turner. Turner was an up-and-coming barrister who would go on to touch silk in 2000. However, he quickly moved up the legal ranks and just four years later, in 2004, he was appointed a circuit judge and then was promoted to Deputy High Court Judge just a few short years after that. Turner currently sits as the Deputy Chair of the Chair of Clergy Discipline for the Church of England.

The defence, unfortunately, relied heavily upon using outdated prejudices to paint Cynthia as an unlikeable woman who took great risks with her personal safety via the promiscuous lifestyle she lived. The prosecution was no better, for they couldn't even offer a motive for the murder. They simply posited that John Taft had visited Cynthia at her bungalow, and sex occurred (whether consensual or nonconsensual, the prosecution never made clear), whereupon John Taft strangled Cynthia. He then stole some of Cynthia's jewellery and car and drove the car eight miles to the Chester High Road, where he abandoned it. He returned home, where he burnt his clothes and buried the remains in the garden. Two days later, he drove the fifty miles to Romiley, where he discarded the stolen jewellery in a phone box. Why John Taft, a man of impeccable and kind character throughout his life, would suddenly do any of this out of the blue was never satisfactorily explained by the prosecution.

Barbara Taft gave evidence. She told the Court that she and John Taft had married in 1974 and had divorced amicably in 1988. She stated that on the weekend of Cynthia's murder, she had been away in Sussex attending a university course. Upon her return, Barbara Taft alleged that John Taft told his wife that he had been at Cynthia's house on the day of the murder carrying out work, and he was concerned he might be accused of the murder. He was so concerned he'd burnt the clothes and shoes he'd been wearing that day. He then asked Barabara to lie and say she had been home with him on the evening of the murder if the police ever asked her.

As Barbara Taft gave evidence, several inconsistencies arose in her story. She'd testified to discussing the photofit with her husband the weekend of the murder. This plainly couldn't have happened as the photofit was not released until several months later. She testified that the police had first interviewed her husband the weekend of the murder, but they had not. John Taft was not spoken to by police until November 1983. In her initial police interview, she stated that she "*gained the impression*" that John Taft had burnt his clothing and buried them in the garden. Now, she was testifying that John Taft had explicitly told her that he had done this. Barbara testified that John Taft had torn pages out of his works diary to destroy any record of his meeting Cynthia via his work. The police had the Birkenhead Glass diary from 1983, and no pages were missing. When Oliver Blunt pulled Barabara up on these glaring inconsistencies, Barbara's only defence was to say that after so much time had passed, *"the memory can play funny tricks."*

Taft's neighbour, Mrs Joan Evans, was called to give evidence. She stated that she witnessed Taft digging a two-foot hole in his garden at around midnight on the evening of Cynthia's murder. She was certain of the date as the family had returned home from a holiday in France that very same day. The prosecution speculated that Taft was burying the burnt remains of his clothing, although they had no physical evidence of this. The police had dug up the garden and used ground penetrating radar, and yet no remains of any clothes were ever found.

Joan Evans' testimony was also contradicted by her own daughter, Sarah. Sarah Evans testified that she too had been looking out of the same window as her mother, and although she did see a man in the Taft's garden, it had been too dark to positively identify him and too dark to see what he was actually doing.

The prosecution claimed that John Taft had fitted a fire canopy for Cynthia on the day of the murder, and this was primarily why he was at her property that evening. The fire canopy was shown to the jury. The prosecution failed to mention that the fingerprints of whoever fitted the fire canopy had been discovered on its reverse side. These fingerprints did not match John Taft's. The prosecution failed to disclose this vital information to the defence until many years after the trial.

John Taft took to the witness stand. He fully admitted spending the evening of Saturday the 8th of October 1983 with Cynthia Bolshaw and that they had consensual sex. Taft stated that he left Cynthia alive and well at 10.30 p.m.

Taft stated that when he found out about Cynthia's murder, he did not approach the police as he was scared that he would be implicated in the murder. The longer he left it, the more he realised how problematic finally admitting to the police that he had been in a sexual relationship with Cynthia would be. Interestingly, Taft testified that Cynthia had a black eye when he arrived at her bungalow that fateful evening, and when questioned about it, Cynthia stated that it was *"one of those silly things."*

John Taft denied burning or burying clothes in his back garden. He did, however, admit to being out in his garden in the early hours of Sunday the 9th of October 1983. Taft's house backed onto the Wirral Way, a 19-mile former railway line that now forms part of the stunningly beautiful Wirral Country Park. The path meanders all the way from West Kirkby at the tip of the Wirral Peninsula down to the village of Hooton near the city of Chester. This country park pathway is a mecca for wildlife. John Taft would often leave food and milk out for the wide variety of wildlife that lived on the Wirral Way but which often found its way into his garden. Several neighbours were called briefly to testify that they had seen Taft many times out in his garden late at night, placing the food out on the lawn for the wild animals.

The defence argued that the whole crux of the prosecution's argument was flawed. Just because John Taft's semen was on the negligee, it didn't follow that Taft murdered Cynthia. Oliver Blunt argued that the semen stain and its position on the negligee were entirely consistent with John Taft ejaculating inside Cynthia during consensual sex. The semen then leaked out of Cynthia's vagina onto the negligee as she sat on the bed. There was other forensic evidence that supported this argument. The fact that there was no urine on the negligee showed that Cynthia had taken it off after the semen stains got onto it. Cynthia, remember, had urinated as she was being strangled. This made it entirely consistent with the murder having taken place several hours after John Taft had left the scene.

The jury retired on Monday the 22nd of November 1999. Twice the jury sent a message to Judge Clarke to state that they were unable to come to a decision. The judge was about to recall the jury and order a mistrial, and the defence was discussing with the prosecution the possibility of Taft being given bail until the second trial commenced. Then, all of a sudden, the jury returned. After three days of deliberation, they were able to come to a majority verdict. Ten members of the jury had decided that John Taft was guilty of Cynthia Bolshaw's murder, and he was duly sentenced to life imprisonment.

John Taft was released from prison in 2012. He is one of the only convicted murderers in the United Kingdom to be released whilst still protesting their innocence. He moved to the Birkenhead area with his wife, Susan. Taft continues to protest his innocence. He said in a 2022 interview with Esquire magazine, *"Think about it. Apparently, I lived as a model citizen for 33 years, committed a horrendous murder, lived another 16 years as a model citizen and then a further 12 years as a model prisoner! Is that really the pattern of a violent man?"*

I tend to agree with John Taft. There were too many inconsistencies in the prosecution's case, unforgivable loose ends, and unanswered questions, which all point to an innocent man having been convicted.

As John Taft's trial progressed, the prosecution received further DNA evidence. This had been a test of a bloodstain on the pillow that had been on the bed where Cynthia was murdered. The DNA result came back as a mixed profile. One set of DNA belonged to Cynthia, and the second set of DNA came from an unidentified female. Not long before her murder, Cynthia had been seen having an altercation with an unknown female who threw a drink over Cynthia and issued violent threats as Cynthia drank in a local pub. Many believed this was the spurned wife or girlfriend of one of Cynthia's lovers. So, Cynthia was known to have a female enemy who was a strong alternate suspect to John Taft. As this would have been hay for the defence to weave very strong reasonable doubt with the jury's mind, the prosecution quietly forgot about this evidence and didn't tell the defence for several years, and only then by mistake. Taft changed his solicitor, and in the bundle of documents handed to the new solicitor was a file the defence had never seen before, containing much new evidence that had been held back by the prosecution.

Remember Mrs Elliott? The neighbour who walked past Cynthia's bungalow at 11.30 p.m. on the evening of the murder. Mrs Elliott stated with certainty that Cynthia's car was still in the driveway when she walked past the house. Thanks to the Evans' evidence, we know that John Taft was seen in his garden just half an hour later. Yet, it would have taken Taft at least two hours on foot to get from where Cynthia's car was abandoned by the A540 back to his house in Heswall.

To get around this glaring omission, Judge Clarke suggested that Taft committed the murder, stole the jewellery and drove home, burned and buried the clothing, and *then* went back to Cynthia's bungalow and stole her car. We then have to believe that after Taft rather pointlessly stole the car and dumped it in a field, Taft then walked a mile along the A540, where he would have been seen by any passing motorists. The passing motorist would have remembered seeing Taft as that particular section of the A540 is a country road with no pavement. He then had to climb a fence and drop down a fifteen-foot embankment onto the Wirral Way, which would have been in pitch darkness. Taft would then have had to have walked a further eight miles home along a precarious country pathway.

Why Taft would do this was never satisfactorily explained because it makes absolutely no sense. There was no rhyme or reason for him to have done any of this. This ludicrous explanation is also contradicted by the claim that brown fibres identical to the ones found in Cynthia's bedroom were also found in the car. Clothes that Judge Clarke wants us to believe Taft had *already* burnt and buried! No, either John Taft murdered Cynthia and miraculously made an 8-mile journey on foot in less than half an hour, or we have three eyewitnesses who prove John Taft couldn't have been the killer.

Then we have that witness who saw the man standing beside Cynthia's car at the scene where it was abandoned on the Chester High Road. Remember that this suspect was described as being mid-fifties with dark, curly hair and glasses. Not at all like John Taft, who was early thirties, blonde and didn't wear glasses.

What about the discarding of the jewellery in Romiley? Well, the prosecution asserted that John Taft had once worked in Stockport, not far from Romiley, and so probably would have known the area well. However, it makes little sense to then say the discarding of the jewellery was an attempt by Taft to throw the police off the scent and look away from the Heswall area, only for him to dump the jewellery in an area that could be easily linked back to him.

If we credit Taft with a little more intelligence, we have to ask why Taft would keep hold of the jewellery for two days. Think of all the incumbent risks that would have brought. Either the police or his wife could have found the purloined goods. Then, after a nervous two-day wait, Taft drove fifty miles just to dump the jewellery in a random phone box in an area that could be linked back to him. Let's suppose Taft was the killer, and he took the jewellery to make the killing look like a robbery that had gone wrong. He then wanted to get rid of the jewellery. Taft could have much more easily taken a quick five-minute walk down to the banks of the River Dee and thrown the jewels into the water, never to be seen again.

What about that stocking mask found in Romiley? John Taft would have had no need to wear such a ridiculous disguise as he was a welcome visitor to Cynthia's bungalow. Given that we can be so sure it was present at the scene when Cynthia was murdered, it would make perfect sense to assert that the killer must have been wearing it over his head as a disguise. This screams the fact that, far from being someone who was welcomed by Cynthia, the killer was, in actual fact, an unwelcome intruder in Cynthia's home, and he wanted to hide his identity.

I think all of the above is enough grounds to say there is reasonable doubt about who killed Cynthia Bolshaw. Yes, DNA proves John Taft was at the scene, but it far from proves he was the killer. The one thing that we can be sure of is that Cynthia Bolshaw was a woman confident in her sexuality and whose sexual allure led to desire and possible jealousy, which in turn led to murder.

Only The Lonely: Avril Dunn

The murder of Avril Dunn is a tragic case that has a haunting quality that makes the case linger in the mind. I think that comes from Avril being a particularly vulnerable victim. Avril suffered from anorexia and weighed just five stone at the time of her death. She also cut a slightly lonely figure.

Avril was born in 1960 and was raised in the Scottish city of Glasgow, but the family moved to Luton, Bedfordshire, when Avril was eleven. In 1980, Avril married, but the marriage was not happy, and just three years later, she and her husband divorced. Not long after the divorce, Avril's mental health severely deteriorated, and she succumbed to anorexia. Her weight plummeted, and she became increasingly infirm. In 1982, Avril was hospitalised due to just how malnourished and infirm she had become. Her recovery was long and slow, but by 1984 Avril was strong enough to leave the hospital and go on holiday with her parents.

By September 1985, Avril was finally eating solid food again and building up her strength, but she was still exceedingly slight and small in stature. She moved in with her cousin, David, and began to try and rebuild her life. Yet, Avril remained a very lonely and isolated young woman.

On the evening of Saturday the 14th of September 1985, Avril decided to escape the confines of the house and go for a few drinks at her local pub, The Heron on the Marsh Farm Estate. Avril's walk to the pub and back home took her past a piece of woodland known locally as 'The Spinney.' Avril avoided cutting through The Spinney as there had been two serious sexual assaults in the wooded area in the previous few weeks. The perpetrator of these attacks had not been caught.

On her way to the pub, Avril stopped off at Five Springs tower block to visit a family who lived there. This family felt sorry for Avril, and they believed that Avril made up excuses to visit them simply for some company. This evening was no different. Avril called to collect some videos she had asked to borrow but then returned a few minutes later and asked if she could pick them up another time as she did not want to risk losing them in the pub.

At 8.30 p.m. Avril arrived at the Heron public house on Bramingham Road. Avril visited the pub several times a week. She was always by herself on these visits, but she tried her best to ingratiate herself with the regulars by playing darts. One of the regulars who Avril played darts with that fateful Saturday evening was a twenty-three-year-old local man by the name of Duncan Jackson.

By 8.45 p.m. Avril was alone and distressed in the pub toilets. A customer came into the toilets and tried to console Avril, but Avril proceeded to have an awkward and confused conversation about liking to watch videos mixed with sentiments about her failed marriage. The customer quickly made excuses and left Avril alone in the toilet, crying.

A little later that evening, Avril was seen standing at the bar talking to Duncan Jackson and another local man named Des King.

The trio then had a game of darts, with Des King acting as scorekeeper. Des King would later say of Avril, "*I don't think any of us knew her at all.*

Basically, I think most of us felt sorry for her in the sense that she always seemed to be alone."

Pub landlord Des Perry noticed that Avril left the Heron at around 10.30 p.m., which was unusual as Avril always seemed reluctant to leave what little companionship she found in the pub and go home. Some explanation might come from the fact that Avril was seen leaving the pub with Duncan Jackson and getting into his car.

They then sat in the carpark talking for some time, but no one appeared to have seen them drive away.

In the early house of Sunday the 15th of September 1985, Jackson's car was spotted by several witnesses driving erratically around the Sundon Park area and a little later in the vicinity of The Spinney.

At 7.30 a.m. on the morning of Sunday the 15th of September 1985, Avril's body was discovered by a dog walker in The Spinney. Avril had been strangled into unconsciousness, stripped naked, raped and beaten. Her death was caused by multiple injuries to the head, neck and chest, the results of being stamped upon. Injuries to Avril's anus suggested that someone had attempted but failed to rape Avril anally. Strangely traces of bitumen[ix] were found on Avril's body.

Detective Superintendent Mel Thompson was placed in charge of the investigation. He set in motion the usual merry-go-round of procedures, house-to-house enquiries, a fingertip search of the local area, and pulling in the local sex offenders, weirdos and snitches for an ear bashing. Several witnesses who were interviewed told the police that Avril had last been seen in the company of Duncan Jackson.

On Wednesday the 18th of September 1985, Avril's missing clothes and handbag were discovered abandoned in a bin on the Marsh Farm Estate.

Avril's skirt had semen stains covering it, and Avril's t-shirt had been slashed with a knife. There were also telltale black stains of bitumen on the t-shirt and around the zipper of Avril's jeans.

Duncan Jackson was the immediate prime suspect.

Whilst he had no convictions of a violent nature on his record, he was known to the police for theft and burglary matters. Whilst not releasing Jackson's name to the press, DS Thompson did release a description and artist's impression of a suspect to the press that looked tremendously like Jackson. DS Thompson stated that the unidentified suspect also drove the same model car as Jackson. This man was said to be key to the enquiry, and anyone with any information about the man's identity should come forward. DS Thompson was essentially telling the local community as openly as he could that he knew that Jackson was the killer, and he just needed people in the local community to come forward and give him the evidence to prove the young man was the killer.

A reconstruction of Avril's last night was filmed and broadcast on national television. In this reconstruction, DS Thompson specifically asked Duncan Jackson to play himself, talking to the actress playing Avril at the bar and playing darts with her. This was no doubt an attempt at psychological intimidation to unnerve Jackson.

Police searched a shed in Sundon Park belonging to Duncan Jackson. Here police found bitumen identical to that found on Avril's body and clothing and a knife with a blade that matched the slash marks on Avril's t-shirt. DS Thompson was convinced that Duncan Jackson had taken Avril to Sundon Park, where they had gone into the shed. At some point, Avril changed her mind about sexual intercourse and told Jackson that she didn't want to have sex with him. Whereupon Jackson had entered into a rage and beat Avril to death before driving her body to The Spinney and unceremoniously dumping Avril in the woods.

The problem was, although it was a rather neat theory backed by some circumstantial evidence, DS Thompson had no way of proving beyond all reasonable doubt that Duncan Jackson had raped and murdered Avril.

The investigation was wound down, and Avril's murder was classified as unsolved. That is until 1998, when a cold case review of Avril's murder was carried out by Bedfordshire Police. The semen stains found on Avril's skirt were tested using techniques not available to the police back in 1985, and low and behold, if the semen didn't contain a DNA profile that was a 100% match for Duncan Jackson. Jackson found himself being arrested and charged with Avril's murder on Monday 14th of September 1998, exactly thirteen years to the day that Avril was so brutally slain.

Duncan Jackson's trial commenced on Thursday the 6th of January 2000, at Reading Crown Court before Mr Justice Garland. Jackson pled not guilty. His defence was that the semen must have gotten onto Avril's skirt when she masturbated him a few days prior to the murder. Jackson stated that he did not tell the police about this sexual encounter back in 1985 as he did not want his wife to find out about his infidelity.

Back in 2000, DNA was a relatively new concept, and the prosecution took pains to explain to the jury how DNA could be used to identify criminals with 100% accuracy. The jury was told in no uncertain terms that there was only a one in a billion chance of Jackson not being the killer. Despite this, the jury was hesitant. Jackson was by now a father of four, a hard-working roofer who had lived a law-abiding life since Avril's murder[x]. Was his story about a sexual encounter with Avril a few days before her murder plausible?

Could his DNA have really gotten onto her skirt via such a loveless transaction? After a long deliberation, the jury returned with a majority verdict of ten to two against Jackson. He was promptly sentenced to life imprisonment.

Despite the conclusive DNA evidence, Jackson continued to deny any involvement in Avril's murder. Nevertheless, Jackson was said to have "impeccable behaviour" whilst being held in prison. Whilst being held at Wormwood Scrubs, Jackson was one of a number of inmates to tackle a fire that broke out in the healthcare unit, and he was commended by the Governor of the prison for his bravery and quick actions. Jackson also undertook anger management and Thinking Skills Programmes and alcohol awareness courses run by the Probation Service. No doubt it had been identified that alcohol had disinhibited Jackson on the night of the murder playing a critical part in Avril's untimely demise.

Between 2004 and 2007, Jackson raised several thousand pounds for Children In Need by running half-marathons. Then, in 2007 Jackson's wife died, and due to an administrative cock-up, he missed the funeral. Despite this, it was noted how Jackson dealt with his grief and his missing the funeral appropriately and calmly. Duncan Jackson was released from prison in 2015.

I'm loath for the last word in this account to be about Duncan Jackson. I want the lasting memory in your minds to be that of poor Avril Dunn. Small and vulnerable, weighing just five stone, all she wanted was a friend and someone she could watch some videos with. Instead, she met a predatory sexual monster. Her lonely life was unfairly and cruelly cut short, but perhaps via this account, we can all become the friend to Avril Dunn that she so desperately wanted in life.

The Murder In The Basement: Violet Milsom

Our next case was described by the Bristol Post as *"pure horror."* The victim was an elderly[xi] lady described as *"a lonely old soul."* She lived alone in the basement flat of 62 Ashley Road in the St Paul's district of Bristol, a city in the South West of England. It was into this one-bedroom slum that a killer crept in the dead of night and did the most unspeakable things to the petrified old dear. It's a haunting case which certainly made an indelible impression on the minds of several young viewers lucky enough to be allowed to stay up late and watch the reconstruction on Crimewatch UK. It was a reconstruction that drew controversy. It led to an angry editorial in that most respected elder statesman of the printed presses, The Times, where the editor foamed at the mouth and asked if the show was *"pandering to a morbid fascination and, in making the subject exciting and interesting, maybe promoting the evil it is trying to fight."* Hysterical? Of course. Yet, I am sure you will see as you read this account why the televised reconstruction unnerved and stayed with those few impressionable young minds.

Violet Milsom was born on Monday the 8th of January 1923, in Bristol. Her stock in trade was as a costumier, in which profession she was listed for several years in the Kelly's Directory for the Somerset District. In her later years, she'd worked in a chicken restaurant but had, by the time of her murder, been retired for several years. As a young woman, she married and had three sons.

By 1985, Violet had been divorced from her husband James for fourteen years, and she was living alone in a *"dingy basement flat."*

It was heavily implied in the press that Violet was estranged from her three sons, and she didn't get to see the grandchildren whose photographs lovingly sat upon her mantlepiece. Indeed, her only company were two cats called Ginger and Tiny. Violet didn't like living alone and was quite a fearful old soul. Each evening Violet put a note in the window of her flat that read, *'**NO** answer after 6 o'clock to **ANYONE**. Thank you.'*

Violet was a woman of predictable behaviours. She would arise early every single day. After washing and dressing, she would go to the shop for her morning papers. Violet would return home and read the papers as she breakfasted. She would then potter around for a few hours, carry out chores or do a bit of shopping before going to the local corner shop around a quarter to five to buy the evening papers. She would then return home in order to (as was always said by people of Violet's generation) get in and get settled. She'd cook herself an evening meal and eat it as she read the evening papers and listened to the soothing classical music played on BBC Radio 3. At 7.00 p.m. each and every evening, Violet would take a sleeping pill and would be in bed fast asleep by 8.00 p.m. Wake and repeat the predictable behavioural pattern every single day.

At around 10.00 p.m. on Tuesday the 3rd of September 1985, Violet was awoken by the sound of breaking glass. Three young men had smashed a pane of glass in her front door in an attempt to break into the flat. Violet was able to scare the men off by shouting that she was calling the police.

Three weeks later, on Thursday the 26th of September 1985, Violet went shopping at a shop called the Trading Post in Stokes Croft, very near to where Violet lived. Violet was looking to buy a chest of draws. Violet couldn't afford the £10 to buy the chest of draws outright, but the owner of the shop felt a little sorry for Violet. He, therefore, allowed Violet to place a deposit down on the chest of draws and promised he would hold on to the item until she could afford the outstanding balance. This in and of itself wouldn't be that remarkable, other than the fact that it allowed the owner of the shop to recognise Violet when he saw her again the following day. She was walking down Stokes Croft with a tall thin man in his early twenties who had long unkempt hair and was unshaven, wearing a cloth cap. Violet seemed to know the man and was animatedly chatting to him.

The next sighting of Violet was on Monday the 30th of September 1985. She collected her £36 state pension from Lower Ashley Post Office and went to do her weekly shopping, spending £5 on groceries. She returned home with her shopping, and her neighbour offered to tend to the garden at the front of the flat. The neighbour didn't get a chance to finish the gardening before being called away on more urgent business, and he promised to return the next day to finish off.

At 4.45 p.m., just as it was starting to turn dark, Violet popped to the local shop to buy the evening paper. This was the last time that Violet was seen alive.

At 8.00 p.m., a neighbour of Violet's, David Crowley, was walking along Ashley Road when three youths came out of the garden at the front of number 62. The three youths pushed passed Mr Crowley in an intimidating manner, and he hurried on home.

At 8.30 p.m., a second neighbour saw a group of four youths loitering at the end of number 62's garden path. Whether these were the same youths who had intimidated Mr Crowley a little earlier or who attempted to break into Violet's flat the previous month, we can not say for sure.

A little later that evening, a neighbour called Pat Abrahams heard "*a lot of shouting and banging*" coming from number 62, but Pat could not be sure if the noises had come from Violet's basement flat.

At around midnight, a witness was walking along the road that ran parallel to Ashely Road. A man stepped out of one of the backyards. He was described as thin, in his early twenties, with collar-length, unkempt brown hair, unshaven, and wearing light denim jeans and a light woollen sweater. Unfortunately, the witness could not be 100% certain if the man had come from the backyard of number 62 or one of the properties on either side. Nevertheless, the police felt that this man was an interesting enough suspect to have two photofits made up of him. Enquiries were made both with the residents in number 62 and in the flats in the buildings on either side. None of the residents recognised the man, and all denied that a man matching his description had visited them on the evening of the murder.

On the morning of Tuesday the 1st of October 1985, a man was seen acting oddly in Ashley Road. He was crying, shouting, "*No! Oh, no!*" And banging his head on a garden wall. For a moment or two, he collapsed into a foetal position on the pavement and was uncontrollably sobbing. When he gathered himself somewhat, the man got up off the ground and began to walk in the direction of Stokes Croft, waving his arms and aggressively punching the air. Residents on their daily commute to work and on the school run gave the "odd man" a wide berth.

About half an hour after the witnesses saw the "odd man," Violet's neighbour called at Violet's flat, intending to finish off the gardening for her. He wanted to borrow a broom so he could sweep up after himself. Instead of finding a broom, he found Violet's body. Violet had been raped, strangled, and her body mutilated with a knife with a 5-inch blade. The exact nature of these mutilations has never been disclosed as the police believe they are too disturbing for public consumption. Violet's hands had been tied using a pink nylon belt that had been brought to the scene by her killer. Police surmised that this belt had probably been taken from a summer dress. A similar ligature had been used to throttle Violet. Strangely, given how stranger averse Violet was, there had been no forced entry into the flat.

A team of 80 police officers was gathered to investigate the horrid murder, headed Detective Superintendent Malcolm Hughes. When it was discovered that Violet's pension was missing, DS Hughes told the press, "*It puts a whole new complexion on the matter. Before, we only knew of a sexual motive. But now we may be looking for a man who is a thief as well as a sexual pervert. What he did to Mrs Milsom was done deliberately and not in the heat of the moment.*"

There was one other item that the killer took from the scene, and it certainly was a very odd thing to take. The killer took with him that odd little handwritten note that Violet placed in the window every evening, warding people away. There is also the possibility that the missing pension was a smokescreen. You see, the killer left behind a considerable sum of money that was in a purse that the killer had clearly found when ransacking the flat but had not taken with him. If the pension was a ruse to make the murder look like a bungled burglary gone wrong, then the motive for the murder was far more chilling and far simpler. It was a sex crime, pure and simple.

There was one oddity found at the scene. A Christmas card from 1976 or 1977 that Violet had kept for some reason. The message on the front of the card read, *"For My Sweetheart At Christmas,"* and the inscription inside the card simply read, *"To Vilet, From Steve."* This baffled the police. Violet's sons couldn't remember Violet having any friends called Steve, and she certainly hadn't dated since her divorce, to the best of their knowledge. This was confirmed by Violet's few friends. They knew of no one called Steve, Violet had never mentioned a Steve, and as far as anyone knew, she'd never dated anyone since the divorce. And yet, the tone of the letter is sweet, loving even. However, would someone in an intimate relationship with Violet have spelt her name wrong? Did you notice that? Steve had spelt Violet's name Vilet. It's hard to imagine spelling the name of someone you were in an intimate relationship with wrongly. There must have been a reason why Violet kept that one solitary Christmas card for nearly a decade when she had discarded all others, even those she received from her family and grandchildren. Whatever the reason, the police never uncovered it.

The police believed there was a witness to the murder. A homeless man by the name of Old Sam would spend his nights in the doorway of the Shady Grove Café, which was directly opposite Violet's flat. There was one problem, Old Sam lived in his own private little world and could not communicate either verbally or in writing. If he had seen the murderer, he could not tell a soul.

House-to-house enquiries were carried out, and 300 posters were put up around Bristol asking for information. Violet's son, Roger, made a public appeal for information, *"Someone in St Paul's must have seen or heard something. I cannot believe that no one knows anything. The whole family is shattered by this. The person who did it must be really sick."*

The investigation quickly ground to a halt, and in desperation, DS Malcolm Hughes took the case onto Crimewatch, where he told the 20 million viewers, *"I've dealt with a number of murders, and without a doubt, this is one of the worst."* Presenter Nick Ross stated that the police were worried about this murder for a particular reason, and he asked DS Hughes if he could explain why to the viewers. DS Hughes replied, *"Mrs Milsom was brutally and sadistically killed. I believe the man who killed her is mentally disturbed and dangerous. I also believe if he's not caught, he may kill again. I also believe somebody knows who he is or may suspect they know who he is. If there is anybody who knows who killed Mrs Milsom or who suspects somebody of killing her, then please come forward and speak to me because they may prevent another terrible crime... I think it's a possibility he will kill again, yes."*

With no real suspects, the police were left only with theories. One police theory was that the man seen with Violet on Friday the 27th of September 1985, the man coming out of the backyard on the night of the murder, and the man seen inconsolably crying the next morning, were all one and the same person. Indeed, the descriptions of these men from the differing witnesses all do broadly tally. Same age, height, weight, same longish unkempt hair, same unshaven appearance. However, it's impossible to say beyond all reasonable doubt if all three siting were of the same man or three completely different men. Several appeals were made for the man or men to come forward and eliminate himself or themselves from the enquiries. He or they never did.

The police never made much headway with the murder of Violet Milsom. There were no real clues or leads that the police could get their claws into and make any sort of case out of. The investigation quickly floundered, and the murder remains unsolved to this day.

The murder of Violet Milsom is a case that few know about outside of Bristol. There are one or two internet forums where the case has been mentioned and two news articles on the Bristol Posts' website, but I could find no podcasts that have ever discussed the case and no YouTube videos where crime buffs pick over its intricacies. Violet Milsom looks in danger of being forever forgotten. That's largely why I chose her case for this book. The women I write about in these pages should never be forgotten. Their untimely deaths should be remembered and talked about. We shouldn't shy away from the evil that men do to such vulnerable women just because the victim doesn't meet certain criteria that might make the case clickbait. I hope, therefore, these few pages

go some way to readdressing the disservice to Violet in her case being so

widely forgotten.

Because She Was A Woman: Diane Sindall

In my hometown of Birkenhead, there is a shrine at the side of the busy main arterial route that takes you from North Wales through Birkenhead and on into the nearby city of Liverpool. The simple black memorial stone reads:

Diane Sindall

Murdered 2. 8. 1986,

Because She Was A Woman.

In Memory Of All Our Sisters,

Who Have Been Raped And Murdered.

"We Will Never Let It Be Forgotten."

This shrine sits at the spot where twenty-one-year-old Diane was slain in a murder so vicious the killer was dubbed *"The Beast Of Birkenhead."* It was a case that loomed large in my childhood and which haunted the town for years after the bloody event took place.

The events began on the evening of Friday 1st of August 1986, in the village of Bebington. Here Diane worked as a barmaid in the Wellington Public House. It was a busy Friday night, and by the time the last customer had left and the pub had been cleaned and tidied, it was 11.45 p.m. before Diane had the opportunity to leave.

Diane was driving a distinctive blue Fiat van that had been given to her by her uncle for use when delivering fruit, vegetables and flowers bought from his greengrocer's shop in Seacombe. It was an old, battered and very distinctive vehicle with lots of unpainted patches of bodywork.

Diane drove along the Old Chester Road towards Birkenhead. Just as Diane reached the usually busy intersection of Argyle Street South, Clifton Crescent, and Borough Road, the van ran out of petrol. Diane was noted for being forgetful and a bit ditsy. Unfortunately, this rather endearing quality would lead to her horrid demise.

At midnight two carpenters working late in the 'Auto' garage[xii] on Borough Road noticed the distinctive blue van pull to a stop outside the shop, and Diane exited the vehicle and set out along Borough Road. It is unclear what Diane intended to do. She had two possible options, walk half a mile along Borough Road to the Shell Garage in the Tranmere area, or walk a little less far to her friend's house off nearby Whetstone Lane.

Although Borough Road is a main road, it is extremely broad and not very well-lit. On one side of the street stood shops which were all closed at that time of the night, and on the side that Diane walked, the pavement was overlooked by the backs of houses that stood on the Woodlands Estate.

At 12.03 a.m., Gary Lamb, the driver of the number 87 Crosville bus that took passengers from Parkgate to Liverpool, saw Diane walking along the road, looking in her bag and looking around her surroundings as if she was looking for someone or something. Diane was alone at this point.

At 12.10 a.m., a taxi driver saw Diane a little further along Borough Road and near to the spot where her body was ultimately discovered. Now Diane was in the company of a man wearing a leather jacket, and they appeared to be arguing, with the man holding his hand out, stopping Diane's progress along Borough Road.

A few minutes later, Diane was spotted again a little further along Borough Road at the junction of Whetstone Lane and Charing Cross. This time she was alone again, with no sign of the man who had been arguing with her a few short minutes before. This was the last time Diane was seen alive.

At noon on Saturday the 2nd of August 1986, a local woman was walking her dog along Borough Road. The dog pulled to go up a little dead-end alleyway at the side of a house that backed onto Borough Road. Diane's body lay naked and abused in the alleyway. At the time, Diane's injuries were so horrific the police refused to release details of them to the public. However, only very recently have they become publicly known. Professor Geoffrey Garrett, the Home Office Pathologist who conducted the autopsy, said of the injuries, "*There are limits, and this was far beyond them.*"

It is not reading for the faint-hearted or those of a sensitive disposition.

Dianne had been stripped naked, and her bra and t-shirt and been wrapped tightly around her neck as if used to throttle her. Scratch marks on her legs, back and shoulders indicated that Diane had been attacked from behind, knocked to the floor and then dragged up into the alleyway. There were three lacerations to Diane's forehead. The first was half an inch long and three-quarters of an inch in width above the right eyebrow and so deep it cut down to the bone. The second in the centre of the forehead was half an inch long, and the third was above the left eyebrow and was one and a quarter inches in length. Both eyes were bruised and cut, and her nose was broken.

The skull had been hit at least four, possibly five times with such force it had, in the words of Professor Garrett, *"crushed like an eggshell at breakfast."* The killer then used the heavy implement to obliterate Diane's face.

The right side of Diane's chin was bruised and lacerated. A deep laceration of one inch in length over the lower jaw was so deep it exposed the bone.

Both upper and lower jawbones were fractured on the right side. The force of the blows had loosened Diane's teeth. There was bruising and abrasions to the neck and larynx and fractures to the thyroid cartilage. The bronchia and lungs contained blood that Diane had inhaled during the attack. Professor Garrett concluded that a heavy object had been brought down on Diane's neck, crushing and bruising the area.

There were bite marks on Diane's breasts. Both nipples had been bitten, with the left nipple being bitten clear off and shoved into her naval. There were defensive marks on Diane's hands. There were lacerations inside and around the vagina, indicating that a heavy object had been used to beat the vaginal region. There were also scratches and abrasions to the stomach, legs, and arms.

The killers' next actions took place a little before 8.00 p.m. on Sunday the 3rd of August 1986, two and a half miles from where Diane's body was discovered, on Bidston Hill. Two dog walkers called Ann Lovern and Jim Foster, discovered a small fire near Viner Road North. Placed on the fire were Diane's clothes, bag, and the burnt remains of Diane's bankbook.

Detective Superintendent Tom Baxter and Superintended Roger Corker were placed in charge of what was to become the biggest murder investigation in

Merseyside Police's history to that point. They immediately began to set out to discover more about Diane and her life to see if the key to her murder lay in her personal relationships.

Diane was a hard-working young woman who, during the daytime, worked for her uncles' greengrocers come florists in Seacombe, and three nights a week, she worked in the Wellington Public House in Bebington, approximately five miles from her home. Diane worked so hard as she was imminently due to get married.

She had been engaged for four years, and every penny the couple earnt was scrimped and saved towards the wedding plans and the life they would have together beyond the wedding day.

Local enquires uncovered a universally loved local lass with no one with a bad word to say about Diane. Of course, the police conducted the usual discreet enquiries and ruled out Diane's fiancé, David Beattie, as a possible culprit or any of her immediate family members.

One of the first mysteries was to try and discover how Diane ended up where her body was discovered. Because, strangely, Diane's body was 150 yards back down Borough Road from where the final sighting had taken place at the corner of Whetstone Lane. This indicated that, for some reason, Diane was heading back to the van without getting either petrol or help. Why?

Had something spooked her, and she thought she would be safer locked safely inside her van? Or had someone offered her a ride?

Once the family had been ruled out, DS Baxter began to investigate a possible link between Diane's case and a seventeen-year-old girl who was sexually assaulted on Borough Road at around the same time that Diane's van broke down. The young girl had been discovered sitting in a very distressed state on a park bench just yards from where Diane's body had been discovered. This avenue of investigation turned into a frustrating dead end.

A further avenue of investigation was a White Ford Sierra seen parked in the bus stop near to the alleyway where Diane was murdered. Public appeals were made for the driver to come forward and eliminate themselves from the enquiry, but they never did.

Publicity for the case was ramped up when on the September 1986 edition of the much-missed Crimewatch UK television programme, there was a reconstruction of the Diane Sindall case. The reconstruction was the main centrepiece of the show, and DS Baxter appeared live in the studio to discuss the case and appeal for witnesses to come forward.

Thanks to Crimewatch, the police got the break they were looking for. An anonymous tipster contacted the show and told the operator that they had seen a very odd man, who they knew only as Peter loitering nervously on Bidston Hill on the evening that Diane's clothes and belongings had been set on fire. Peter regularly drank in The Crown Public House on Conway Street in Birkenhead and was on the darts team there. Undercover police conducted discreet enquiries at the Crown Public House, and they discovered that the most likely suspect was a twenty-nine-year-old pub regular and darts team captain called Peter Sullivan.

On Thursday the 25th of September 1986, police conducted a search of Sullivan's home address in Queensbury Garden's in Birkenhead, where they discovered a two-foot-long clawed crowbar.

Professor Garrett conducted a forensic analysis of the implement and concluded that it was the murder weapon.

When confronted with these facts, Peter Sullivan broke down and confessed to Diane's murder.

Just who was Peter Sullivan, and why on earth did he murder Diane? Well, Peter Sullivan was one of life's losers. As a child, he had been severely bullied. At one point, he had been hospitalised when older boys had forced him to swallow metal nuts and bolts. He wasn't academically bright and failed his secondary exams. Indeed, as a mark of how woefully unintelligent Sullivan was, I have had an urban myth about Sullivan positively confirmed by two separate sources. The first source was Sullivan's regular appropriate adult, who was brought in by the police to look after Sullivan's best interests whenever he was arrested.

Sullivan's appropriate adult just so happened to be my mentor when I was reading law. The story was also confirmed by Professor Garrett, the Home Office Pathologist who conducted the autopsy on Diane. Both men stated that Sullivan once stole a car, the car broke down, and Sullivan flagged down a police car to give him a jump start.

Yes, Sullivan was *that* thick.

Unskilled and finding it difficult to learn new skills, Sullivan became a labourer. Unhappy with his life, Sullivan retreated into a fantasy world where he told people he was highly skilled, super intelligent and much more important than he actually was.

He told people he was friends with famous people. He told people he'd had professional trials for Wolverhampton Wanderers. None of it was true. He ended up living with a much older woman in a maisonette in Queensbury Gardens, Birkenhead, and the couple had a son.

From an early age, Sullivan had also entered into a life of petty criminality. Sullivan even stole from his own parents. Sullivan accrued eighteen convictions for petty offences but none for violence. Before Diane's murder, Sullivan had wasted five years of his life serving the occasional short-term prison sentence.

Early in 1986, Sullivan began to regularly drink in the Crown Public House on Conway Street, Birkenhead. Sullivan couldn't help but lie to the people who drank in the pub, and he began to tell them that he was such a good darts player he could go professional. He told the other regulars that professional darts players Eric Bristow and Jocky Wilson were his personal friends, and both had encouraged him to go pro. All this boasting led to Sullivan being appointed the captain of the Crown's darts team. Friday the 1st of August 1986 was the first match where Sullivan was captain, and the Crown's team was roundly trounced. The visiting darts team made a holy show of Sullivan and showed everyone he'd spent months boasting to just what a liar he was.

After the match, Sullivan smarted. He got uproariously drunk, and when the pub closed, he sullenly slinked off back home. Back at Queensbury Gardens, Sullivan continued to fester. He resolved that someone should pay for his humiliation, and to that end, he armed himself with a two-foot metal crowbar and stalked off into the night, heading towards Borough Road, where he had the fateful meeting with poor Diane Sindall.

When Peter Sullivan came to trial at Liverpool Crown Court in October 1987, Sullivan retracted his previous confession stating that he had been intimidated by the police and had been forced into making the confession. He now wished to plead not guilty to Diane's murder. However, expert evidence given by an orthodontist left little doubt in the jury's mind that it was Peter Sullivan who had bitten off Diane's nipples and that his teeth marks were as unique as his fingerprints.

On Tuesday November the 3rd 1987, the jury retired to consider their verdict, and after a perfunctory discussion and a leisurely lunch, the jury returned with a guilty verdict. Mr Justice Temple called Diane's murder *"a crime of considerable abomination and outrage"* as he sentenced Sullivan to life imprisonment. In February 2022, the Ministry Of Justice confirmed that Peter Sullivan *"is likely to die in prison."*

The murder of Diane Sindall is a case I have wanted to write about for many years. Yet, the almost mythical status the crime has in my hometown stopped me from doing so. I was keenly aware that any attempt to write about Diane's case could appear ghoulish or disrespectful, and as my long-term readers know, that is something I have always tried to avoid being in every single one of my true crime books. However, in this very special edition of Murder Tales, where the victims are the most important part of the retelling of the events, I felt Diane's story needed retelling, for as her memorial says, *"We will never let it be forgotten."*

The Beauty In The Bikini Murder: Ann Heron

Yes, this is another 'beauty in' murder, a tabloid phrase trotted out whenever an attractive woman is murdered in unusual circumstances. Indeed, this next case has some similarities to the murder of Cynthia Bolshaw but is unique enough on its own merits to be of interest to any adherent of true crime. When I think of murder, I usually think of darkness, nighttime, cold weather, outdoors, a slight mist, and the smell of autumn in the air. I don't know why, but that's the scene that is automatically conjured up in my mind when I think of such dreadful deeds. Of course, this would be entirely erroneous. Most murders occur inside the victim's home and can occur at any time of the year. Our next case took place during a blazing heatwave when the attractive victim just happened to be sunbathing in her garden.

Mary Ann Heron nee O'Neill was born in Glasgow on Sunday the 24th of March 1946, to William Patrick O'Neill and Margarette O'Neill nee Tarrier. Known as Ann to her friends, she married her first husband, a police officer called Ralph Cockburn and settled in Dorchester Avenue in the Anniesland district of Glasgow. The couple began a family, and before too long, the couple had two sons and a daughter, Ralph Jnr, Michael and Ann-Marie. Seeking a quieter life, the family ultimately moved to the picturesque Isle of Bute.

In 1979 Ann began an affair with a forty-two-year-old businessman named Peter Heron. They met whilst Peter was on a golfing holiday on the Isle of Bute, and Ann was making a bit extra pocket money as a barmaid at the Golf

Club. Peter had been married to his wife Catherine for twenty years, and they also had three children, Debora, Jacqui and Beverly. After the golfing holiday ended, Ann and Peter stayed in touch. Peter came from Darlington in the Northeast of England, where Ann just so happened to have a friend. When Ann went to visit her friend, she met up with Peter, and feelings between them grew. Eventually, Ann and Peter fell madly in love with one another. When they were genuinely convinced that their relationship wasn't merely a product of the boredom that often creeps into long-term partnerships, they both reached a unanimous decision to leave their families behind and embark on a new life together. This just so happened to coincide with Peter getting a much better-paid job as the managing director of Stiller's Transport, a haulage and logistics firm.

In 1982 the couple bought Aeolian House. A large, isolated, detached house set in grounds off the A67 road, a mile from the town of Darlington and a few short minutes' drive from the offices of Stiller's Transport. Then, in 1986 Ann and Peter married at Yarm Road Methodist Chapel in Darlington, followed by a lavish reception at nearby Wynyard Hall. However, over time Ann grew unhappy. She missed her children, whom she'd left behind in Scotland. Ann's daughter, Ann-Marie, said that the last time she saw her mother, "*there was sadness in her eyes.*"

Friday the 3rd of August 1990 was the hottest day of the year, with temperatures reaching 98°F or 37°C. Ann Heron had spent the morning shopping with her friend Dawn Perry. Ann was due to attend an 18th birthday party that evening, and she wanted to buy a special gift for the special birthday. Ann returned to Aeolian House at around midday.

Every day Peter Heron would return to Aeolian House for lunch with Ann. They ate together, and then Ann changed into a bikini and stepped out into the garden to sunbath as Peter Heron left to return to the office, by now it was approximately 1.50 p.m. Ann's friend, Sheila Eagle, telephoned Aeolian House at 2.30 p.m., and Ann chatted to Sheila on the telephone until approximately 3.00 p.m.

Ann then went back outside and lazed on a recliner at the front west corner of Aeolian House. Ann would normally have sunbathed in the privacy afforded at the back of Aeolian House, but a neighbouring farmer was digging up his field using a tractor, and it was causing great clouds of dust to travel across the grounds of Aeolian House. At around 3.30 p.m., Ann was spotted sunbathing by Margaret Shaw, who was passing Aeolian House on a bus that was travelling along the A67. For many years this was officially the last time that Ann was seen alive.

Peter Heron returned to Aeolian House at 6.00 p.m. As Peter drove up the driveway, he noticed that the front door to the house was wide open, and the dog was sitting outside. Ann had left the radio playing on the floor next to the sun lounger, and there was a half-smoked cigarette in an ashtray and a half drank glass of wine. Peter entered the house and walked into the lounge, where he found Ann lying face down on the floor. Ann's throat had been slashed numerous times using either a Stanley knife or razor blade. Her bikini bottoms had been removed, and she had been sexually assaulted.

Peter telephoned the police and then his boss Paul Stiller and asked him to come to Aeolian House. Stiller arrived at Aeolian House before the police. He found Peter in a distressed state outside of the house and stood beside his car. Peter asked Stiller to "*go into the house, Paul, and then come out and tell me it isn't true.*" Stiller went into Aeolian House only to return moments later himself visibly shaken, and he embraced Peter to comfort him.

When the police arrived, Peter attempted to follow the uniformed officer into the lounge again. The officer stopped Peter and asked him to wait outside with Stiller. Detective Superintendent Keith Readman was put in charge of the investigation. He quickly ruled out robbery as the motive, as nothing had been disturbed in the house, and nothing had been stolen. Police searched the grounds of Aeoline House with metal detectors to try and find the murder weapon. It was never recovered.

There were few forensic clues. An autopsy carried out by Home Office Pathologist Dr James Sunter revealed that Ann had died at approximately 5.00 p.m. that fateful Friday. Peter's bloody fingerprints were found on the telephone in the hallway and on the roof of his car. These were all entirely consistent with Peter having got blood on his fingers when he touched his wife upon first coming across the body and checking to see if she was still alive. The only anomaly, as far as the police could see, was that Ann's shoes, a bottle of suntan lotion and the book she had been reading were approximately fifteen metres away from the sun lounger, placed on the ground under a tree.

Other than sex, the murder appeared motiveless. Obviously, the police considered Ralph Cockburn and Peter Heron's ex-wife as possible suspects, but both had moved on and were now happily settled in new relationships. More importantly, both had cast-iron alibis. Peter Heron also had a cast-iron alibi; he had been in Darlington in front of a room full of business executives heading a crisis meeting at Cleveland Bridge & Engineering Company, a client of Stiller's Transport. With no obvious suspects, the police began to consider that perhaps a passing motorist had seen Ann sunbathing in her bikini, and the said motorist had become overcome by a manic sexual desire. Had rape led to murder?

Police set up roadblocks on the A67 and began to question all motorists. Over a thousand questionnaires were sent out to local residents, asking them for any information whatsoever. The usual house-to-house enquiries were carried out, and these tactics bore rich fruit.

Several witnesses had seen a white or silver coloured car driving at high speed around the country lanes surrounding Aeolian House between 3.50 p.m. and 4.50 p.m. on the day of the murder. This car had been rhythmically flashing its headlights at other drivers as they passed. One of the witnesses stated that the driver of the car was an older gentleman wearing dentures and that these were quite clearly *"swishing around the driver's mouth."* One witness believed the erratic driver may have been Peter Heron. However, Peter's alibi and the fact that he did not wear dentures ruled him out.

Two friends of the Heron's came forward and stated that at 4.15 p.m. that Friday afternoon, they had been driving past Aeolian House and had seen Ann sitting in the driver's seat of a blue car signalling to turn into the driveway. The witness flashed the headlight of their HGV lorry at Ann, and she smiled and waved back. Ann had two passengers in the car, one sitting in the front passenger seat with his hands on the dashboard and one sitting behind Ann. One witness remembered commenting to the other, "*Ann must have friends or relatives down from Scotland for the weekend.*" The witnesses remembered the sighting vividly for several reasons. Firstly, Ann was not in her own car, but a strange blue one. Secondly, on the parcel shelf in the rear window of the car, there was a distinctive 'object' that was the 'trademark' prop of a well-known local DJ who compared in Darlington nightclubs. The police have never revealed what this object was. Asked by the press how certain the witness was about the sighting, the witness replied, "(I am) *adamant, 100% certain, that it was her.*" The witnesses could identify Ann with such certainty because they were both very good friends with Ann's daughter, Ann Marie. Bizarrely, the police never revealed this sighting to the public, and it was left to one of these witnesses to go to the press several years later to tell the world how the Durham Police had seemed disinterested in the information they had to offer.

The sighting of Ann sitting in a blue car is important when taken in conjunction with other witnesses. A witness came forward to state that they had seen a blue car, possibly a Vauxhall Astra, parked outside Aeolian House at about 4.45 p.m. This was then confirmed by two other separate witnesses. A neighbour called Liz Lamb came forward to state that she had seen the same blue car speeding out of the driveway of Aeolian House at around 5.05 p.m. The car then sped off "*at ridiculous speed*" down the A67. "*They wanted to get away from that house quick,*" Liz would later tell journalists. A taxi driver confirmed this sighting and told the police that, for a moment, he thought he was going to collide with the car as it came out of the driveway. Both Liz and the taxi driver described the driver of the blue car as being a suntanned male, aged between thirty-five and forty-five, with short dark hair.

This was clearly seen as an important lead because DS Readman made an urgent appeal for the driver to come forward and eliminate himself from the enquiry, "*Please someone come and tell us who that blue car belonged to, who was in the blue car, and what on earth took that blue car up to Aeolian House.*" The police even began to try and track down the driver of every blue car in the country and eventually interviewed the owners of 3,500 blue-coloured cars. Police even took several of these witnesses around local car showrooms to see if they could identify the make and model of the car that they had seen so they could narrow down the search.

In the years since, several writers, journalists, and the families involved have queried why the police never produced an artist's impression or photofit of this important suspect. Despite the fact that, at the time, the police said that Liz Lamb and the taxi driver both described the car and driver almost identically, Durham Police Constabulary now says, "*The descriptions of both the vehicle and the person driving the vehicle differ and lacked the detail required for a photofit.*" To anyone who has read the original news reports or seen the highly publicised reconstruction, this is clearly poppycock and smacks of someone trying to justify the blinkard misdirection that the investigation ultimately took.

A further witness came forward to state that at around 5.00 p.m., she saw a man running away from Aeolian House in the direction of the village of Middleton St George. The man struck the witness as odd because he was running in long trousers during a stifling heatwave. Another witness came forward to tell the police that they had seen a dark blue Sherpa van with a distinctive trident design painted on its side door parked at the end of the driveway of Aeolian House facing towards the road. The van was stationary, with three men sitting in it. The police appealed for the running man and the men in the Sherpa van to come forward, but none of them did.

In the days after the murder, a Darlington resident, who had a telephone number very much like that of the incident room, received a misdialled telephone call. At the end of the line was a very distressed woman who said she had vital information about Ann's murder. The person receiving the erroneous call gave the distressed woman the correct number for the incident room. So unnerved by the tone of the call, the recipient of the wrong number contacted the incident room themselves. The distressed woman never did contact the incident room. However, in October 1990, Ann's murder was prominently featured on Crimewatch UK. Again, a woman in a very distressed state telephoned the TV studio and told the telephonist that she had vital information about the murder. The caller hung up before she could speak to one of the officers involved in the case. The police appealed for the woman to come forward and tell them what she knew. She never did.

Four days after Ann's murder, the police held a press conference at Darlington Police Station, where Peter Heron appealed very calmly and emotionlessly for any witnesses to come forward, *"I want to appeal to the ladies and gentlemen of this country to find this man. There must be somebody sitting with him today. There's a possibility that this man could do it again."* DS Readman also told the press, *"This was a savage attack with a fiendish weapon to cause such an injury."* He also admitted that the police had very little to go on. After the press conference, Peter Heron and his daughter Debbie were privately told by a publicly unidentified police officer that if the case wasn't solved within the next two weeks, then they should prepare themselves for the case going unsolved.

A week after the murder, the police discovered something which changed the whole focus of the investigation. Police were informed that Peter Heron had been having an affair with a thirty-two-year-old barmaid who worked at Dinsdale Spa Golf Club, where Peter Heron was a member. However, the affair had ended several months before the murder. Peter Heron would later say of the affair, "*It wasn't serious. It wasn't going to become serious. It was something that happened that I didn't expect to happen... It was something we drifted into.*" Indeed, the other woman stated that she and Peter Heron only had sex on two occasions and that calling it an affair was too strong a term, "*fling would maybe probably be a better word than an affair.*" The fact that the affair was over didn't matter. Peter Heron now had to be considered a suspect with a strong motive.

Four weeks after the murder, Peter Heron had the keys to Aeolian House returned to him by the police. Heron's daughters agreed to go and tidy up before Peter Heron moved back in. As they were cleaning and tidying the room where Ann had died, Heron's daughter, Debbie Simpson, looked out of the window and saw a blue car parked on the road outside the house. The male driver appeared to be staring at Aeolian House. Debbie telephoned the police, but filled with adrenaline, Debbie rushed out of the house and ran over to the car to confront the driver. He was a suntanned male, in his thirties, with short dark hair. The car window was down, and the sun-kissed driver was smoking a cigarette. Debbie demanded to know what the man wanted, and he replied, *"That man ruined my life."* Debbie Simpson recognised the man immediately; it was the husband of the woman Peter Heron had been having an affair with. Despite being told about this incident, and it being confirmed by Peter Heron's lover, the cuckolded husband was never considered a murder suspect by Durham Police. Durham Police stated that the cuckolded husband had been interviewed and gave an alibi that appeared to be satisfactory, and so they concluded that his description and car matching the suspect seen on the day of the murder was purely a coincidence.

By 1994 the investigation was effectively dormant, then in October of that year, letters started to arrive on the doormats of the key players in the investigation. They were sent to Peter Heron, Darlington Police Station, and the Northern Echo, a local newspaper that had tried to keep the story in the public eye. Four letters were sent over an eight-day period, all posted in the Darlington area. One of the letters sent to the Northern Echo read:

"Hello editor it's me Ann Heron's killer! I'm _(OOO)_ . I enjoyed it so much. I love hurting people physically and mentally I've dropped them bastards at Parkgate[xiii] a line and have sent Peter Heron letters explaining myself (I don't owe anyone any apologies).

Your readers will have plenty to talk about

Signed - The Killer ††"

The police were not inclined to take the letters as genuine but did concede that the letter they received (which they have not released to the public) described the murder scene in *"vivid and authentic detail."* The memory of the Wearside Jack hoax during the Yorkshire Ripper enquiry was still fresh in the police's collective memory, and they were loath to make the same mistakes again, wasting manhours investigating a potential hoax. Nevertheless, the police appealed for the letter writer to come forward and identify themselves. Of course, they never did. Because of the lack of effort in investigating the letters, it is still up for debate as to whether they were genuinely sent by the killer or whether they were a particularly cruel and sick hoax.

By 1995 the police had interviewed 9,000 people, 4,000 witness statements had been taken, and 5,500 lines of enquiry had been followed up, alongside 1,200 forensic samples being collected and analysed. More than 100,000 hours had been spent on hunting Ann's killer. The case had ground to a halt, and the active enquiry was wound down. Both Peter Heron, his family and Ann's children from her first marriage have both said that police communication was abysmal and that from just a few short weeks after the murder had taken place until 2005, they had no further contact with Durham Police.

In 2000, Detective Superintendent Keith Readman retired. During a retrospective interview about his career with a local journalist, Readman was naturally asked about the only unsolved murder in County Durham history, that of Ann Heron. DS Readman stated that it was still his belief that the murderer had been the driver of the blue car seen speeding away from Aeolian House. He told the journalist, *"If they* (the witnesses) *had even seen part of the* (number) *plate, the murderer would have been detected because I am confident this was the man who killed Ann."*

Peter Heron tried to move on with his life. Two years after Ann's murder, he married a widow called Freda Buddie, whom he met via his work. Freda felt sorry for Peter Heron, who had become a very lonely and isolated figure since Ann's murder, and Freda invited Peter to dinner. This simple act of kindness led to romance and, ultimately, marriage. The marriage was a happy and loving one, and in 2000 Peter Heron retired, intending to spend the rest of his days with Freda. Unfortunately, not long after Peter retired, Freda was diagnosed with cancer, and she passed away in July 2005.

As Peter Heron cared for his dying wife, Durham Police carried out a cold case review on the Ann Heron investigation. Microscopic traces of DNA from semen discovered at the back of Ann's throat were tested using the latest forensic techniques, and finally, they were able to get a DNA profile. It was a 100% match for Peter Heron. On Wednesday the 9th of November 2005, Peter Heron was arrested and charged with Ann's murder.

Peter Heron protested his innocence. So confident was he that the police would realise that they had made a mistake that he refused to be represented by a solicitor during the ten hours of police interviews that followed. Peter Heron answered all of the police's questions, he didn't go 'no comment' or pretend that he didn't remember details because of the passage of time. He was nothing but open and seemingly honest with the police. The obvious question of how his semen got onto the back of his wife's throat had an all too obvious answer. He and Ann enjoyed an active sex life, and Ann had orally pleasured him shortly before her murder.

Indeed, by this point, Ann's son, Ralph Cockburn Jnr, was a serving police officer himself. When he was told how dubious the evidence the police had gathered against Peter Heron was, his immediate thought was, "*Well, that's not going to stick.*" Nobody could believe that Peter Heron was being charged with his wife's murder on such flimsy evidence. Indeed, a journalist called Kevin Donald, who had followed the case from the beginning, called the decision "*perplexing.*"

At a Magistrates committal hearing, the lay bench remanded Peter Heron into custody. He was duly taken to Holme House Prison. However, when a second bail application was made to a Crown Court Judge in chambers a week later, the judge found the case against Peter to be weak and the grounds for bail being refused spurious. The judge granted Peter Heron bail pending trial.

On Thursday the 9th of February 2006, there was a hastily convened pre-trial case management hearing. The CPS told the bench that a senior barrister had been briefed to prosecute the case. Barrister Portia Ragnauth had reviewed the evidence. Ragnautha subsequently informed the CPS that it was her expert opinion that the case against Peter Heron was nowhere near strong enough to secure a conviction. She had therefore recommended that the trial be vacated. The Crown Prosecution, therefore, made an application for the charge of murder to be withdrawn. Neither the police nor the CPS had the good grace to tell Peter Heron or his legal team about this hearing. Peter had to find out from journalists who door stopped him. Peter Heron subsequently had his solicitor, Peter Wishlade, release a press statement where he called the whole charade "*a malicious prosecution… and at this moment consideration in connection with a civil claim is being considered."*

For Peter Heron, the damage was done. He said that friends he'd had virtually all his life abandoned him overnight after his arrest. He's stated several times to the press that he feels he is stuck in limbo, with the cloud of suspicion still hanging over his head and no possibility of his finally clearing his name beyond all reasonable doubt in a court of law. Ann's son, Ralph Cockburn Jnr, was pragmatic about the prosecution being dropped and supportive of Peter Heron, *"From a professional point of view, I knew that that was the best thing. I didn't want somebody convicted who the evidence wasn't there to convict. I want the person who killed my mum caught and convicted."*

I don't believe Peter Heron murdered Ann. One of the most persuasive pieces of evidence that brings me to this conclusion is that when the police arrived at Aeolian House, Peter Heron was wearing the exact same clothes he'd been wearing all day. A white shirt and beige trousers. The killer would have undoubtedly been covered in blood. This evidence alone should rule out Peter Heron as a suspect. Apart from that easily explainable semen at the back of Ann's throat, there was not a single shred of evidence against Peter Heron other than an easily disprovable witness sighting of Peter Heron driving towards Aeolian House at around about the time Ann was murdered. This witness made several glaring errors in their statement, which brings the whole veracity of their evidence into question. This sighting of Peter also can not be squared with Peter having been in that meeting at Cleveland Bridge & Engineering Company.

If Peter Heron didn't murder Ann Heron, then who did? Well, there have been several theories over the years, only one of which I find in any way persuasive.

The first theory is one that has plagued the dafter and darker fringes of internet messaging boards and comments sections. It is that tawdry and well-trotted-out theory that seems to perennially appear when a murder goes unsolved. It is that tired and well-worn old cliché, the Masonic Conspiracy Theory. This baseless theory seems to have emerged for two reasons. Firstly, several of those involved in and around the case and investigation were Freemasons, including Ann's ex-husband, several of the investigating officers, and a swathe of their social circle. Secondly, Ann's throat was cut, which is an ancient masonic penalty for betraying the fraternity. Of course, there is no evidence to support this theory at all. It's all just groundless rumours and innuendo that percolates nastily in the grubbier parts of the internet. I mention it here simply for completeness and so that there can be no allegations that I am colluding with dark forces to cover the truth. I think we can happily leave this silly theory here without saying any more about it.

In 2010 a woman who was identified to the press only as Sylvia came to the police with intriguing new information. Sylvia worked in a card shop in Newton Aycliffe, a village approximately eleven miles from Aeolian House. She stated that in either late 1992 or early 1993, a rep for a card company came into the shop and went into the back office with the manager to discuss business matters. Ten minutes later, the rep left the shop smirking, and the manager left the office in a distressed and shaken state. The manager told Sylvia that the rep had just confessed in great detail to Ann's murder and had stated that the police would never catch him as he was emigrating to Australia. Sylvia urged her manager to go to the police, but she refused. Sylvia stated that she was only contacting the police herself after all those years because the manager of the card shop had recently died, and she felt she could finally go against her wishes and tell the police the strange story.

I don't believe this story for a minute. If it did happen, it was probably someone about to leave their job just pulling the leg of someone they didn't like. When asked why a potential killer would suddenly randomly confess to the manager of a backwater card shop, all Cynthia could think of by way of explanation was that the manager looked vaguely like Ann and that perhaps this had stirred some feelings of guilt within the killer. No, for me, this just seems too ludicrous to be true. I think in the Sylvia theory, we have a well-meaning but misguided witness on our hands here.

In 2014, private investigator, criminologist and university lecturer Jen Jarvie contacted the Heron's to see if they would like her to look into the case pro bono. Examining the crime scene photographs, Jarvie concluded that the killer was "*Somebody who was comfortable going into somebodies home. I knew that I was looking for a serial criminal. Somebody who had that propensity to begin with and who may well have done it again.*"

During her investigation, Jarvie was approached by a former convict. He had been a cellmate of a man named Michael Benson. This old lag told Jarvie that Michael Benson had made a jail cell confession to murdering a woman in Darlington in 1990. Benson said he had been in the Darlington area looking for a house to rob when he came across a large, detached house set back some way from the main road. Benson had stated that he had found the owner in the garden at the back of the house sunbathing and that he *"Just did her and went."* There was only one unsolved crime in the Darlington area that could fit this description, the murder of Ann Heron.

So, who was Michael Benson? Well, he was a violent career criminal described by prison psychiatrists as *"manipulative and psychopathic."* He was predominantly a burglar, but he also had numerous offences of violence littering his antecedent history, including offences involving bladed articles. At the time of Ann Heron's murder, Benson had been on the run from the police. Benson had escaped from Leyhill Prison whilst serving a life sentence for Grievous Bodily Harm with a shotgun. Benson was also known to be driving his wife's blue Ford Orion, which looked very similar to the Vauxhall Astra. Benson had family who lived in the Durham area who might have been willing to hide their fugitive relative. Benson also fits the description of the man seen in the blue car. He had tanned skin and was forty years old with short dark hair.

Unfortunately, Benson was unable to be questioned as he died in 2011. However, his ex-wife, Ruth Bennett, was still alive. Journalist Mike Ridley tracked Ruth down and showed her the letter that had been sent to the Northern Echo by the supposed killer. Ridley reported Ruth Bennett's response thusly, *"Upon reading it, the colour drained from her face, and she said: 'One hundred per cent that's Michael's handwriting. I'd recognise it anywhere, and I'd swear on the Bible that he wrote it. I'm convinced he's a killer'."*

After a four-year investigation, Jarvie handed her findings over to the Durham Constabulary in 2018. The Durham Constabulary didn't seem to do anything with the information. When the Heron family kept putting pressure on the

Durham Police for an update, they replied back with a prepared statement in May 2022 that said, amongst other things, *"Michael Benson is not and never has been a suspect"* and that they were *"all but certain"* Benson was living *abroad at the time of the attack."* They further asserted that they had used Benson's familial DNA and compared it to samples found at the crime scene, and they had not been a match.

This raised the question of which DNA samples the police were referring to. As far as anyone had ever been aware, the only DNA sample the police had found was the sample of Peter's semen found at the back of Ann's throat. Was there other DNA found at the scene that the police had not disclosed for some reason? Not even disclosed to Peter Heron's legal team when he was charged with the murder. With these serious allegations being levelled at the Durham Police Constabulary, they referred themselves to the Independent Office For Police Conduct in April 2022. This is the public body that investigates allegations of police misconduct and corruption. Durham police have since remained silent on the subject of Ann Heron's murder.

Durham Constabulary say that the investigation into the murder of Ann Heron is open but inactive. This means they are no longer actively investigating the crime. Of course, they claim they will investigate further if the public brings to their attention any new evidence. However, given the uninterested and, indeed, hostile response that Jen Jarvie got when she attempted to do so, I find this claim to be slightly disingenuous. Friends of Peter Heron and the family of Ann Heron desperately want the killer to be caught and believe that one day the truth will come out, *"You've got to have hope,"* Ralph Cockburn Jnr said recently, *"You've got to have hope that it's going to happen and one day, one day, we will get closure."* Those who follow such cases professionally, such as journalist Kevin Donald are of the belief that we will never see justice for Ann Heron, *"It would take something really unexpected now to solve this case,"* Donald said in 2022, *"If it was a shock that Peter Heron was arrested and accused of murder, it would be an even bigger shock if there was a strong, tangible development now."*

The Plumstead Ripper: Rachel Nickell, Samantha and Jazmine Bissett

This next murder tale is a story about police failure. It's a story about criminal profiling and its dangers. It's a story about dogmatic beliefs and blinkard thinking derailing opportunities that could have saved lives. It's the story of three murder victims killed by the same man; one victim became a household name, and their murder was a national water cooler moment. The other set of arguably more brutal murders went ignored by the press, and even to this day, if you mentioned the victim's names to a random person on the street, they'd stare at you blankly. This is the story of the Plumstead Ripper and, more importantly, his victims.

Rachel Jane Nickell was born on Saturday the 23rd of November 1968, to Andrew and Monica Nickell. She grew up in the affluent village of Great Totham, Essex. It was a privileged upbringing; Andrew Nickell was the chief executive of Ackroyd's Of London, a successful high-end shoe manufacturer. The family lived an idyllic country lifestyle and could afford to own a second home in Devon for holidays and short breaks away.

Rachel was a studious child who passed her 11+ and attended Colchester Grammar School For Girls. She excelled in school, passing both her GCSEs and A-Levels with flying colours, and went on to read English Literature and History at university.

As a youth, Rachel dreamed of becoming a professional ballet dancer. She took lessons at the Essex Dance School, where she proved adept on the dance floor. However, a growth spurt in her teenage years left Rachel too tall to become a professional ballet dancer. Nevertheless, Rachel had lots of other interests that occupied her time. She loved riding horses and swam for England in national competitions. She also had a love for amateur dramatics and acted in several plays at school.

While paying for her university tuition by working at Richmond Swimming Pool as a lifeguard, Rachel was to meet the love of her life. André Hanscombe was a semi-professional tennis player and tennis coach who was visiting the baths with his two younger brothers, Mohan and Chan. Like Rachel, André was good-looking and sporty. The two hit it off immediately. Within a few months, they had moved in together, and within a year, Rachel was pregnant.

Initially, the couple decided that they weren't ready for children and opted to have an abortion. André borrowed the money for the procedure from a friend. However, as the friend handed the money over, he warned André that he and Rachel shouldn't rush into such a huge decision. After a few days of soul searching, Rachel and André decided to keep the baby. If Rachel was going to be a mum, she decided that the new baby would be paramount among her priorities, and so she dropped out of university before finishing her degree.

Rachel, André and Alex lived in a two-bedroom flat on the third floor of Elmfield Mansions, Balham. André had bought the property rather cheaply shortly before the 1987 stock market crash. At the time of purchase, he'd hoped to flip the property over for a quick profit, but the property market was yet to fully recover. So, he and Rachel decided to move into the flat and make it their family home. André had taken on work as a courier to make ends meet while Rachel looked after baby Alex. When Rachel got some free time, she undertook voluntary work for a local charity that cared for disabled children and vulnerable adults.

Rachel had never really recovered from her dreams of becoming a ballet dancer coming to a premature end. She hadn't known what to do with her life for several years. Slowly, she decided that she wanted to try and break into television and become a TV presenter. More specifically, she wanted to become a children's TV presenter. Rachel was exceedingly beautiful and had taken on several modelling jobs, building up a professional portfolio that she hoped would sell her great beauty and warm personality to prospective TV producers. Everyone who met Rachel agreed that she had that rare combination of exceedingly beautiful looks, great intelligence and a naturally warm, excitable, larger-than-life personality. It was just going to be a matter of time before a television executive spotted this winning combination, and Rachel would undoubtedly be propelled to great stardom.

On Wednesday the 15th of July 1992, Rachel, Alex and Molly, the family's pet dog, decided to go for a walk on Wimbledon Common. Rachel drove her silver Volvo Estate and parked it in one of the public car parks near Windmill Wood. She arrived at the common at approximately 10.00 a.m. Wimbledon Common is a thousand-acre parkland filled with ponds, woodland, and lovely walks. Before that day, it was seen to be one of the safer parts of London; it was for this very reason that Rachel had begun to use Wimbledon Common for her regular walks with Alex. Although Wimbledon Common was slightly further from her home, men pestered her on the much closer Clapham Common and Tooting Bec Common. These negative experiences culminated in a man exposing himself to Rachel on Tooting Bec Common. After this, Rachel decided to walk in the safer environs of Wimbledon Common.

As Rachel and Alex entered a secluded woodland just 300 yards from the carpark, the killer struck. He picked up Alex and threw him into some brambles. Then he turned his attention to Rachel. Rachel was stabbed forty-nine times. At least thirteen of the stab wounds had been inflicted post-mortem. The wounds to her neck were so severe her head had almost been severed from her torso. The initial stab wound to the neck had killed Rachel instantly, as attested by the lack of defensive wounds. Her killer then dragged Rachel twelve feet away from the path into the seclusion of some trees, stabbing her as he went. The killer continued to stab Rachel as he removed her jogging bottoms and undergarments. The killer sexually assaulted Rachel and inserted something into her anus. Semen stains were identified on Rachel's jogging bottoms, from which the police were later able to retrieve a DNA sample. After killing Rachel, the killer rifled through her purse. He didn't take anything, but he did remove a folded piece of paper on which the PIN number for Rachel's bank card was written. The killer had laid the piece of folded paper almost gently onto Rachel's temple[xiv].

At 10.35 a.m., a retired architect called Michael Murray was walking his dog when he came across the scene. Initially, he thought Rachel was sunbathing, *"As I got closer, I realised this was something quite different and horribly tragic,"* Murray would later say. Alex was hysterical in distress, clinging to his mother's body and begging her to wake up. Mercifully, Alex hadn't been hurt physically by the killer. However, he had watched as his mother was brutally murdered and sexually assaulted. It took a psychological toll on the young boy, who became largely nonverbal for quite some time afterwards.

The police were immediately called, and Superintendent John Bassett was placed in charge of the investigation and assigned fifty detectives to investigate. They closed off the common and began a search. The people who had been on the common were only allowed to leave once they had given a police statement.

Despite the fact that 500 people were on Wimbledon Common at the time of the murder, few people had seen anything suspicious. Detective Inspector Keith Peddar, a newly promoted officer from the Flying Squad, who was ultimately given the job of evaluating any potential suspects, was surprised by how few witnesses there were, *"The fact that we had no one coming forward saying that they had actually seen a bloodstained man decamping from the Common surprised me. It struck me that whoever was responsible for this had had the luck of the devil."*

There had been a handful of potentially useful witness sightings. At approximately 10.40 a.m. Amanda Phelan saw a man bending down at the side of a path about 150 yards from where Rachel was murdered, washing his hands in a ditch. He was described as being twenty to thirty years of age, six foot tall with short collar-length hair, wearing a cream sweater or shirt and loose-fitting blue jeans and carrying a black bag. Upon seeing Ms Phelan, the man made off quickly in the direction of Putney Vale Cemetery. Police discovered a pair of distinctive size nine footprints at the spot and had the foresight to make a plaster cast impression of them. These footprints matched exactly a set of footprints that were found by Rachel's body.

Jane Harriman had been walking the common with her two children. They had seen a man who fitted the same general description, complete with a black sports bag, with the added detail of his having a "*babyish face*" and "*stooping gait.*" Curiously, this man's belt was fastened around his shirt at mid-stomach height as opposed to being looped around his trousers. This peculiar man was seen loitering around the Windmill Car Park. The man left Ms Harriman and her children feeling nervous and apprehensive, and they noted that he appeared to be following a blonde-haired woman at a distance. This woman was later identified as not being Rachel but Iris Imbert, the wife of Sir Peter Imbert, the Commissioner of the Metropolitan Police Force.

Mrs Harriman and her children saw the same man at around 10.15 a.m. from a little distance off, walking around a spot called the Curling Pond, heading toward Windmill Wood, where Rachel's body was discovered.

The police became convinced that both witnesses had seen the same man. This, when combined with Alex giving the police a description of the killer via a child psychologist that roughly tallied with these witness sightings, led the police to firmly believe the man in the white shirt with the black sports bag was the killer.

Another witness came forward to state that around 10 30 a.m., they had been driving along the A3 when they saw a man wearing only a pair of boxer shorts and carrying a bundle of clothes running across the road away from Wimbledon Common towards the Roehampton Estate. The man was tall and thin, in his thirties, with a mullet hairstyle. The police concluded that this man had nothing to do with Rachel's murder, but they appealed for him to come forward in case he had seen something of vital importance. They even had an artist's impression of the man made up, which the police released to the press.

In the immediate aftermath of the murder, at around midday on the 15th of July, police guarding the murder scene stopped a man from moving too close to the closed-off area. The police officer felt that the man was acting suspiciously, and she asked for his name, and he told her it was Colin Stagg. The man asked what was going on and why the woods were closed off, and after being told about the murder, he moved off.

Forensic Pathologist Dick Shepherd carried out the autopsy. He told the police that the weapon used was a knife with a blade approximately 1.5cm in width and 9cm long with one cutting edge. Dr Shepherd estimated that the time of death was around 10.35 a.m. If Michael Murray had arrived at the scene a few moments earlier, he no doubt would have come face to face with Rachel's killer. Dr Shepherd stated that due to the angle of the cuts and slashes, he believed the attacker had been standing either behind or to the side of Rachel.

André Hanscombe was devastated by Rachel's murder. He simply couldn't contemplate life without Rachel. Come the morning after the brutal event, André had resolved to kill himself and Alex. He explained the situation to his infant son as best he could. Trying to put it in terms he could understand by explaining that one day, Molly, the dog, would be too old to want to play and carry on. Alex spoke for the first time since the terrible event, simply saying, "*I want to go on, Daddy.*" André realised that he couldn't kill himself, let alone his two-year-old son. They would somehow get through this traumatic experience together. Building a life that would honour Rachel and make her proud.

The case received massive press interest. Detective Chief Inspector Michael Wickerson would later say, "*The public response to this is something I've never seen before.*" In part, this was due to Rachel being an incredibly attractive young woman with model-good looks. In part, it was due to the particular brutality of the murder. In part, it was because the murder had taken place in broad daylight in a nice, fashionable, middle-class area. Within days of the murder taking place, the News Of The World newspaper put up a £15,000 reward for anyone who gave the police information that led to a conviction. To try and capitalise on the press interest, André Hanscombe was asked to take part in a press conference. A police officer discreetly held André's hand under the table as he emotionally told the waiting journalists, "*This person has to be found before someone else is killed and another family destroyed.*"

Police had an artist's impression drawn up of the man seen by the witnesses on Wimbledon Common. When it was released to the press, it got an immediate response; at least four people in the local neighbourhood put forward the same name, Colin Stagg.

As the investigation seemed to run aground, it was the Association of Chief Police Officers who suggested to Chief Inspector Michael Wickerson that he should consult with Paul Britton. Britton was a forensic psychologist with a history of helping police with complicated investigations. His role was usually to come up with an offender profile of the person responsible for the crime. Profiling is the process of identifying the psychological characteristics of a suspect and then forming a general description of their personality based on the analysis of the crime scene and the perpetrator's actions when committing the offence. Britton also advised police on how best to effectively interview suspects using psychology to manipulate the interviewee into opening up and disclosing more and more about their crimes.

Most notably, Britton worked with the police during the Fred and Rose West investigation, the investigation into the murder of Jamie Bulger, and the investigation to capture the kidnapper/murderer Michael Sams. Over several years, Britton had built up a formidable reputation for creating offender profiles that were eerily prescient when the killer was eventually caught, and he'd become respected amongst many senior officers who had been initially sceptical about the use of offender profiling.

At the time, Britton worked for the Trent Regional Psychology Service at Arnold Lodge Psychiatric Hospital in Leicestershire, and he was invited down from Leicestershire to the incident room in Wimbledon. Here, he viewed all the information the police had available about the crime. He was shown all of the witness statements and the crime scene photographs. He was taken to the murder scene at Wimbledon Common. After a detailed conversation with DI Wickerson, Britton was eager to help. He could see that the investigators were in dire straits with no leads to follow. He returned to Leicestershire and duly worked up a profile. Britton stated that Rachel's killer would:

- Be aged between twenty and thirty.

- Will have practised the offence, but this will have been his first murder.

- Will have poor heterosocial skills and an inability to relate to women on an ordinary level.

- He will have a history of failed or unsatisfactory relationships, if any.

- Have some form of sexual dysfunction, i.e. impotence or a history of premature ejaculation.

- Use pornography in his sexual fantasy life, some of it probably violent.

- Be of average intelligence and education and be seen as a low achiever.

- Will be untidy and disorganised.

- Live a relatively isolated life and will be single.

- If he is employed, it will be low-skilled or manual labour work.

- Will live either with his parents or alone in a bedsit.

- Will have solitary hobbies and interests, most probably of an unusual nature. May have an interest in martial arts.

- Will not have access to a car.

- Will live locally within walking distance of the murder scene and have a detailed knowledge of Wimbledon Common.

- Will have a significant history of sexual offending but might not have been caught.

Britton concluded that the killer was suffering from *"sexual psychosis"*, someone with strong sexual needs and desires but poor confidence and self-esteem and an inability to interact with others socially. He ended his report with the chilling sentence, "*It is almost inevitable that this person will kill another young woman at some point in the future as a result of the strong deviancy and aggressive fantasy urges.*"

As with all major murder investigations of the time, Rachel's murder was featured on Crimewatch UK. Rachel's murder was the lead segment on the Thursday the 17th of September 1992 edition. Host Nick Ross told the public that the crime was proving "*extremely hard to solve*" and, as a result, the investigators were "*Putting all their cards on the table.*" Ross told the viewers about the suspicious man in the white shirt with the black bag and implored him to come forward. Then he revealed that the police had consulted Paul Britton and that a psychological profile had been drawn up. Key points from Britton's profile were given to the public. There were some points highlighted that weren't in the official profile, most notably stating that for several days after the murder, the killer would have been upset or excitable. His family certainly would have noted a change in his mood and probably would have suspicions about their guilt. Ross told the public that the Crown Prosecution Service had guaranteed immunity to anyone who had previously harboured the killer or who may have been worried about being convicted of minor offences if they came forward.

Superintendent John Bassett appeared on the show. He appealed directly to the killer's family, "*I believe a mother, sister or girlfriend knows the identity of this man. Women have an instinct for men that are odd like this. This man is dangerous, and he's ill. He needs attention."*

The appeal had a massive impact. Over 800 phone calls came into the incident room from the public, who were only too eager to help. Four separate callers all had concerns about the same local man, Colin Stagg. Notes were checked, and it was realised that Stagg's name had come up several times in relation to the photofit. Not only this, but they also discovered the report from the uniformed officer about Stagg loitering suspiciously near the murder scene on the afternoon of the murder.

Police checked their records. Colin Francis Stagg was a man with no criminal record or history of being suspected of any crime. He was twenty-nine, unemployed and, importantly, a virgin. The product of a broken home. His father had brought him up after his mother walked out on the family in 1975. Stagg had lived alone ever since his father died of cancer in 1986. He was buried in Putney Vale Cemetery. Stagg identified as adhering to the Wiccan belief system or modern-day witchcraft. One room in his flat was painted black with a large pentagram on the wall, and on the front door of his house, there was a sign that read '*Christians Keep Away, A Pagan Dwells Here.*" Keith Peddar was excited by the new suspect, later saying, "*Quite clearly, we were dealing with a very unusual individual.*"

Stagg was placed under immediate police observation. It was nearly twenty-four hours before Stagg left his flat in Ibsley Gardens on the Roehampton Estate. When he did, and the officers saw the striking similarity Stagg bore to the photofit image, the decision was made to arrest him for Rachel's murder immediately.

Stagg was taken to Wimbledon Police Station, where Detective Inspector Keith Peddar interviewed him. The interview took place over two days. Stagg believed he was being as open and honest as he could. He believed he was voluntarily giving the police a wealth of information they could use to exonerate him, although Stagg freely admitted later, "*I was getting more and more frightened, and I couldn't think of anything coherent to say. So, my words were being mixed up and that was being used against me. I couldn't think clearly... It was just, really, a stressful time.*" The police had a different perspective on the interviews. They believed Stagg was being deliberately difficult and evasive, "*It was very, very difficult to pin Colin down to answer specific questions,*" Keith Peddar said, "*You would ask him a question, put something very pointed to him, and he would come up with the most illogical response by way of answer.*"

Stagg stated that on the day of Rachel's murder, he had been crippled by a migraine. He had taken his dog, Brandy, on a short walk early in the morning on the common, starting at about 8.15 a.m. While on the common, the only person he saw was a dark-haired woman with her hair up pushing a buggy, being followed by a broad man with short dark hair who was "*quite a menacing looking bloke.*" Stagg then returned home, arriving at about 9.15 a.m. Stagg stated that after sleeping on the settee for a few hours, he had felt a little better and so took his dog on a slightly longer walk on the common, where he had spoken to the police officer about the murder.

When asked what he had been wearing on the day of the murder, Stagg stated that he had been wearing a black t-shirt, cut-off short jeans and a black leather jacket. He said he had been wearing white trainers, but the police wouldn't be able to compare these to the footprints found at the scene as he had thrown them out two days after the murder.

The clothes Stagg had been wearing on the day of the murder were of vital importance. After the Crimewatch broadcast, one of Stagg's neighbours, Susan Gale, contacted the police to state that she had seen Stagg starting his walk on Wimbledon Common on the morning of the murder. They were deeply concerned as Stagg had been dressed identically to the man in the artist's impression: long jeans, a white shirt and no jacket. Ms Gale also stated that Stagg had been carrying a black bag and appeared to be in an excited and agitated state. Gale put the sighting of Stagg at 9.30 a.m. Gale was absolutely certain of the day and time of the sighting as she had been rushing home so that she could take her mother-in-law to collect her pension. This sighting was seemingly confirmed by another neighbour of Stagg's named Lillian Avid, who placed her sighting of Stagg going onto Wimbledon Common at 9.25 a.m.

On Sunday the 19th of September 1992, Stagg was placed in an identity parade at Brixton Police Station. The witnesses who had seen the man in the white shirt with the black bag acting suspiciously all picked Colin Stagg out as the man they had seen. When Stagg was told that the witnesses had picked him out, Stagg made a startling confession, not to Rachel's murder, but to exposing his genitals to women on Wimbledon Common. Stagg was charged with indecent exposure and held in a cell overnight. The next day, he appeared at

Wimbledon's Magistrates Court, where he pleaded guilty to the indecent exposure offence and was fined £200.

After his court appearance, Stagg was released on police bail pending further investigation into Rachel's murder. Stagg was allowed to leave the Court via the back door. However, someone had tipped the press off. He was deluged by a wave of reporters wanting a statement. Stagg made an instant bad impression on the public by swearing his way through the crowd, shoving cameramen and sticking up two fingers at a camera crew from the national news. The newly convicted sex offender came across as nasty and thuggish as he swaggered off back home. The following day, national newspapers ran with screaming headlines such as '*Pevert Back On Rachel Common*" next to a photograph of Stagg looking particularly aggressive.

What followed has become infamous in policing circles and led to the use of forensic psychologists and criminal profiling becoming discredited in the United Kingdom. Struggling to find any solid evidence that would convict Stagg, Chief Inspector Michael Wickerson and Paul Britton worked on a plan to get Stagg to incriminate himself. The plan was essentially one long, devious mind game played against an unwitting Colin Stagg. Codenamed Operation Edzell, an undercover police officer would befriend Stagg and develop a relationship with him where he would be encouraged to confide his deepest innermost fantasies and secrets. Paul Britton described the operation as being like a series of ladders whereby Stagg would eliminate or implicate himself via his own choices.

The hope was that Stagg would not only implicate himself further in Rachel's murder but may even voluntarily offer up physical evidence of his guilt, *"The idea was to obtain evidence; physical evidence would have been ideal,"* Keith Peddar explained, *"The knife used to murder Rachel with her blood and his fingerprints on. Clothing that he had worn on the day with Rachel's blood on. That would have taken the enquiry to another level."*

The officer chosen for the undercover operation was a young female officer codenamed Lizzie James. She was selected as she bore more than a passing resemblance to Rachel. James was seconded from SO10, the Metropolitan Police Force's covert operations group. She was an officer who regularly went undercover in criminal gangs and even terrorist cells, assuming different identities for long periods. James had several meetings with Paul Britton at Arnold Lodge Psychiatric Hospital, where they went over the operation. They practised telephone calls where Britton pretended to be Colin Stagg, and they wrote mock love letters to each other in character as Stagg and Lizzie James.

James was given a cover story of being a survivor of ritual abuse at the hands of a satanic coven. As part of her fabricated history, James had witnessed and taken part in ritual murders. Britton reasoned that James could use the emotional upset of this experience as an explanation for why she did not want to rush into a sexual relationship. It was also believed that this esoteric element would prove alluring to Stagg, who had a strong interest in such occult matters. Britton estimated that the undercover operation would take between twenty-four to twenty-six weeks to complete.

Lizzie James first wrote to Stagg on Tuesday the 19th of January 1993. James claimed to have gotten Stagg's details from an old pen pal of Stagg's called Julie Pine. Pine had first approached the police after Stagg's very public arrest. She thought the police would be interested in some of the old letters Stagg had written to her where Stagg had graphically detailed some of his sexual fantasies. Stagg fantasised about being naked and masturbating on Wimbledon Common and having a woman stumble across him. Instead of being frightened, the woman became sexually excited and had sex with him. Pine had been disgusted by the graphic nature of the letter and had ended communications with Stagg, but she had kept the letters. This gave the police the in-roads they needed to start communications with Stagg. The initial letter from 'Julie James' read:

"Dear Colin

I hope you are not offended by this intrusion, as we have never met before, but I feel that I have known you for years. You may remember writing to a woman called Julie; Julie was an old friend of mine and a little old-fashioned in her outlook if you know what I mean. A while ago, whilst she was out, I read a letter that you sent her. This letter has been on my mind and interests me greatly. I find myself thinking of you a lot. I would be very interested in getting to know you more and writing to you again."

Stagg wrote back immediately. In his reply, Stagg said that he liked to sunbathe naked on Wimbledon Common and grumbled that some people found the activity perverted. Paul Britton advised on a reply, which was duly sent. The next letter from Stagg took things up a notch and contained a sexually explicit fantasy about having sex in his back garden. He stated that he got a sexual thrill from the thought of his neighbours seeing them together.

The next letter contained another fantasy of outdoor sex. This time in a park. This fantasy piqued the interest of the police as it seemed to describe the site where Rachel Nickell had been murdered, including details that hadn't been released to the press. When Lizzie James wrote back, she introduced the idea that she wanted to be *"defenceless and humiliated."* Stagg seemed to take to this idea like a duck to water. Stagg wrote back:

"You need a damn good fucking by a real man, and I'm the one to do it... I'm the only man in this world who's going to give it to you. I am going to make sure you are screaming in agony when I abuse you. I am going to destroy your self-esteem. You will never look anybody in the eyes again."

Over the next few letters, Stagg introduced elements of bondage, sexual violence and gang rape. Then, Stagg introduced the idea of using a knife and self-harm during acts of sex. Stagg claimed to be turned on by the idea of Lizzie rubbing blood into her nipples as they copulated. Paul Britton felt that this was a clear indicator of the sexual deviancy exhibited by Rachel's killer.

The undercover operation evolved from letter writing to phone calls to face-to-face meetings. The first face-to-face meeting took place in Hyde Park on Thursday, the 20th of May 1993, Colin Stagg's 30th birthday. Detective Inspector Keith Peddar and Detective Inspector Mick Wickerson observed from an unmarked police van as Stagg watched Lizzie James from a distance for some time before finally approaching her. They spent an hour in a café. James attempted to gain Stagg's trust by giving him a birthday present, a personal stereo and a baseball cap. Then, they discussed their pasts. Stagg told James that he had been accused of murdering Rachel, and James told Stagg that she had ritually murdered a pregnant woman and a baby.

A few days after the meeting, Stagg telephoned James and confessed to murdering a woman with his cousin when he was a teenager. He claimed to have buried the body in the New Forest, Hampshire. The police checked the details of the alleged murder and found that it had been an invention. Stagg and James met again on Friday, the 4th of June 1993, where James quizzed Stagg about the murder. Even though the police knew the murder had never taken place, they wanted to get Stagg used to James' questions in case they ever got to a point where she could quiz him about Rachel's murder.

At a meeting on Wednesday the 9th of June 1993, James finally brought the conversation around Rachel Nickell. Stagg denied having murdered Rachel but described in vivid detail what he had seen in a crime scene photograph the police had shown him during his police interview and admitted to becoming sexually aroused at the content of the photograph. Crucially, the police believed Stagg had told James details about the body that it had not been possible to see in the crime scene photograph.

Further letters followed between the pair in which Stagg detailed violent sexual fantasies involving knife play and blood. Paul Britton felt that these new fantasies confirmed that Stagg had a serious sexual deviance and were also an indicator of latent sexual aggression.

At a meeting in Hyde Park on Wednesday the 21st of July 1993, Stagg and James once again discussed Rachel's murder. Once again, Stagg told James details about the body that the police felt Stagg could not have known unless he had been at the scene, such as the position of Rachel's hands and the fact that there was dilation of her genitals after death.

Something then happened that made the police realise that Operation Edzell was on a hiding to nothing. Colin Stagg did an interview with the Daily Star where he vehemently denied all involvement in Rachel's murder. After this interview was published, the police felt that Operation Edzell had run its course. The information gathered as part of Operation Edzell was given to the Crown Prosecution Service for review. They agreed that Colin Stagg had disclosed enough knowledge that only the killer would have known to charge him with Rachel's murder.

On Tuesday the 17th of August 1993, Colin Stagg was arrested and charged with Rachel Nickell's murder. During further police interviews, Stagg refused to answer any questions. Paul Britton suggested confronting Stagg with Lizzie James. This, it was hoped, would shock Stagg into answering their questions. Lizzie James was brought into the interview room and introduced herself for the first time as an undercover police officer, *"There was a look of shock on Colin's face,"* Keith Peddar said, *"And that was quickly replaced by what I would describe as anger."* Lizzie James said to Stagg, *"Isn't there anything you want to say to me, Colin? It'll be your last opportunity."* Stagg continued to reply with no comment to all questions.

On Thursday the 17th of February 1994, there was a committal hearing at Wimbledon Magistrates Court before stipendiary magistrate[xv] Terry English.

Usually, these proceedings are quick administrative affairs to confirm that the case will be heard at the Crown Court and consider matters of bail. The committal hearing for Colin Stagg turned into a mini-trial that lasted eleven whole days, with several witnesses being called to give evidence. The defence hoped that at this committal hearing, they would be able to prove to Terry English that Colin Stagg had no case to answer and have the whole prosecution thrown out of court.

Firstly, several witnesses testified who identified Stagg as the man they had seen acting suspiciously on Wimbledon Common on the morning of Rachels' murder. Several shopkeepers were called to state that they had seen Stagg on the day of the murder in an excitable state, eager to talk about the murder. Then, several of Stagg's neighbours were called who stated that Stagg had been out walking his dog as early as 8.50 a.m. and heading towards Wimbledon Common at around 9.30 a.m. This cast doubt on his migraine alibi and his assertion that he had not been well enough to go on the long walk that would have led him to the scene of Rachel's murder.

Pathologist Dick Shepherd issued a blow to the defence when he told the jury that the killer would not necessarily have been covered in blood as much of it had soaked into Rachel's clothing. Then Paul Britton gave evidence, telling the jury how the undercover operation had originally been devised to eliminate Stagg from the murder enquiry. Under cross-examination, Britton was forced to admit that there was *"academic concern"* about the practice of offender profiling and that the science was still in its *"early stages."*

Lizzie James then gave her evidence, detailing her months of trying to lure Stagg into confessing to Rachel's murder. Surprisingly, she was given quite an easy time by the defence, who appeared to be keeping their powder dry for trial properly.

The defence's hopes of having the case dismissed came to nothing. Terry English not only committed the case for trial at the Old Bailey, but he once again refused Colin Stagg's bail.

Colin Staggs's trial commenced at the Old Bailey on Monday the 5th of September 1994, before Mr Justice Ognall. Harry Ognall wasn't your typical High Court Judge. He came from a lower-middle-class family that heralded from Leeds. He'd not been educated at a private school but instead passed his 11+ and attended Leeds Grammar School. From there, he read law at Lincoln College, Oxford, where his hard work earned him a scholarship to the University of Virginia School of Law. He was called to the bar in 1958 and touched silk in 1973. Ognall made his name by successfully prosecuting Peter Sutcliffe, the Yorkshire Ripper. He'd been awarded a High Court judgeship in 1986.

John Nutting QC conducted the prosecution aided by junior counsel William Boyce. Nutting was cut from classic high-class barrister cloth. The son of Sir Anthony Nutting MP, he was educated at the exclusive Eton public school and went on to read law at McGill University in Montreal. He was called to the bar in 1968, and from 1976 onwards, he slowly climbed his way up the ranks of the Treasury Counsel to become the First Senior Treasury Counsel, whereupon he touched silk[xvi]. He would ultimately be appointed a High Court Judgeship and become the most senior judge on the isle of Jersey.

Nutting had misgivings about the case against Colin Stagg. He could see that the evidence was all entirely circumstantial and weak circumstantial evidence at that. In the weeks leading up to the trial, he'd had several fraught private meetings with Superintendent John Bassett, Inspector Keith Peddar and Paul Britton in his chambers, where they had discussed the case against Colin Stagg. During these meetings, Nutting let all three know that without the evidence from Operation Edzell, Colin Stagg had no case to answer.

William Clegg QC conducted Stagg's defence aided by junior counsel James Sturman. Clegg is one of Britain's leading criminal barristers. Clegg read law at Essex University before being called to the bar in 1972. During his career, Clegg was involved in several high-profile cases, including defending Michael Stone when he stood trial twice for murdering Lin and Megan Russell, defending Barry George when he was accused of murdering Crimewatch UK presenter Jill Dando, and Vincent Tabak for the murder of Joanna Yeates.

The trial began with William Clegg arguing that the evidence of Lizzie James was inadmissible because her actions had effectively been a honey trap. Colin Stagg was a twenty-nine-year-old virgin who would have said anything to try and bed the attractive undercover police officer. It was an undercover operation that was flawed not only legally but morally. He argued, "*It is difficult to imagine an operation more calculated to result in material which a court would hold inadmissible... Lizzie James subjected Stagg to quite deliberate manipulation designed to get him to incriminate himself.*" Nutting's response to these serious accusations was rather weak, "*The object was not to trick the defendant into making admissions but rather to investigate the defendant's sexual fantasies.*"

After two days of Clegg and Nutting arguing about the legality of the undercover operation, Mr Justice Ognall said that he needed to retire to consider both sides of the argument. When he returned, his judgement was scathing of the Metropolitan Police and their tactics. Ognall angrily eviscerated Operation Edzell and the officers who masterminded it, "*This behaviour betrays not merely an excess of zeal but a blatant attempt to incriminate a suspect by positive and deceptive conduct of the grossest kind... A sustained enterprise to manipulate the accused, sometimes subtly, sometimes blatantly, and designed by deception to manoeuvre and seduce him to reveal fantasies of an incriminating character and to wholly unsuccessfully admit the offence... If a police operation involves the clear trespass into impropriety, the court must stand firm and bar the way.*"

Lizzie James' evidence was ruled inadmissible. Without it, there was no case against Colin Stagg. The trial collapsed, and Mr Justice Ognall ordered Stagg to be released immediately. As Stagg left court, he was met by a large, angry crowd screaming, "*Hang him! Guilty! Hang Him!*"

In the days that followed, the Metropolitan Police went on the defensive. The most expensive criminal investigation in British legal history, costing £3 million, had come to nought. An internal review of the investigation was carried out, which concluded that there was strong circumstantial evidence that indicated that Colin Stagg was Rachel's killer. The Metropolitan Police subsequently released a statement to the press stating that they were "*not looking for any other person in connection with Rachel's murder.*" In other words, they were telling the public that Colin Stagg had done it. They just couldn't prove it.

Paul Britton felt that he was hung out to dry by the Metropolitan Police as they let him take the public flax for the failed investigation. He was vilified in the press; he was portrayed as a power-hungry Svengali pulling the strings of gullible police officers whom the new science of offender profiling had beguiled. Ordered by the Metropolitan Police not to speak publicly about the case, when Britton refused to give interviews to tabloid newspapers, they threatened to destroy his life and air all his dirty laundry in public. Yet, Paul Britton obeyed the order from the Met and remained publicly silent on the matter. The press then misportrayed this silent obedience as Britton displaying a sense of shame or even guilt at having allowed a clearly guilty and dangerous man to escape justice and walk the streets.

The allegation of murder and subsequent collapsed trial ruined Colin Stagg's life. The majority of the country believed he was guilty of murdering Rachel. Several books about the Rachel Nickell case were published in the aftermath of the collapsed trial, which all pointed the finger at Stagg. The wider public and most true crime buffs believed Stagg had gotten away with murder thanks to incompetent police work and clever, unscrupulous lawyers. I'm sad to say I was one of those people who, for many years, believed Stagg was the guilty party.

The public perception of Colin Stagg being Rachel's killer wasn't helped by senior police officers giving rather injudicious interviews. Detective Inspector Keith Peddar went on prime-time TV and said, *"Colin Stagg has been through a version of justice, albeit truncated, and he has been found not guilty. But I wonder whether he can actually say, hand on heart, that he believes people who meet him in the street believe that. I do not believe the system served anybody that particular day."*

Stagg found himself unemployable, abused and spat at in the street. He found his flat regularly vandalised. Youths would throw eggs at his front door on an almost daily basis. He was forced to move several times. In a vain attempt to improve things, Stagg unwisely took part in an interview with hard-hitting investigative reporter Roger Cook. Cook revealed to the public for the first time that Stagg might not have been convicted of violent offences, but he had once stabbed his brother with a pair of secateurs. As Stagg protested that this incident was taken out of context and blown out of proportion, insisting that he wasn't a violent man, footage played off Stagg attacking a cameraman who had doorstepped him in the street with a chain dog lead. Cook confronted Stagg with a litany of inconsistencies in his story. He said to Stagg, *"There have been so many untruths, so many lies told. Perhaps you don't know the difference between the truth and a lie."* Stagg eventually lost his temper with Cook and his aggressive line of questioning and angrily snapped, *"The police are dirty bastards, you know that. They set people up. They change their statements so they can set people up. Everybody knows that."*

Stagg went on to take a lie detector test. He passed the test with flying colours, but it didn't stop people from believing he was guilty. However, he caused further damage to his cause by refusing to answer questions under hypnosis, and he also refused to take a 'truth drug.' Rather than help prove his innocence, such public stunts just made people believe even more that Stagg was a cold and calculating killer, enjoying himself as he gloated in the media spotlight.

As the Colin Stagg debacle played out at the Old Bailey and in the tabloid newspapers, another group of detectives not too far from Wimbledon were having their own problems with an equally complicated murder investigation.

Samantha Bissett was born in Dundee, Scotland, on Saturday the 25th of February 1967, but was raised in Gloucestershire. The only child of Margaret and Douglas Bissett. Her father was a journalist and watercolour artist who died of lung cancer when Samatha was fourteen. Margaret subsequently decided to return with Samantha to Dundee, where Margaret went on to marry a man named Jack Morrison, who was a builder with a successful local business.

The death of her father seemed to affect Samantha deeply. Formerly a diligent and high-achieving pupil, her grades suddenly started to slip. This was compounded by Samantha being bullied for her English accent and middle-class manners. She ultimately left school without obtaining her secondary qualifications. Samantha left school and joined a community of travelling hippies. She lived for a time in a Tippie in south Wales. For a time, she worked as a care assistant in Salisbury. Then, she became a nanny for a woman called Anne Hesketh, but she ultimately lost this job due to Mrs Hesketh discovering that Samantha was regularly abusing drugs.

In 1988, Samantha entered rehab in Southampton. Here, she met a Social Worker named Andrew McNeil. They entered a relationship and moved in together. Like Samantha, Andrew came from a good middle-class background; his father was a barrister, and his mother was a schoolteacher. Samantha fell pregnant, but by then, she had relapsed back into drug misuse. This put a strain on the relationship, and Samantha and Andrew separated. Samantha left Southampton for Woolwich, where she met a man named Conrad 'Cosy' Ellam.

Samantha and Cosy started to date, and Samantha was given a council flat at 1a Heathfield Terrace, Plumstead, southeast London. Not long after taking receipt of the flat, Jasmin was born on Monday the 21st of August 1989. Jazmine's birth was the steadying factor that Samantha needed, and she was able to kick her drug habit. Samantha and Cosy had a loving relationship, and he treated Jazmine like she was his own daughter, but he never moved in with Samatha, choosing to remain living with his parents in Sidcup, Kent.

By 1993, Samantha was making some money as an artist's model and ultimately hoped to make it in the world of glamour modelling. She'd paid for professional photographs to be taken to send out to talent scouts, newspapers and magazines. Samantha was looking to somehow find the funds to educate Jazmine privately at a boarding school in Sussex. She'd made enquiries with the school about part paying the school fees by working as a teaching assistant at the school. Samantha had always been too proud to accept money from her mother and stepfather and didn't want their help paying for the school fees. However, Margaret and Jack wanted Jazmine to have the best life possible, and in the Autumn of 1993, they insisted on paying for Samantha, Cosy and Jazmine to go on an exotic holiday to Gambia. They were due to travel on Thursday the 11th of November 1993.

At 7.00 a.m. on Thursday 4th of November 1993, Cosy called into 1a Heathfield Terrace on his way home from his night shift at a local factory, hoping to spend a few hours with Samantha and Jazmine. 1a Heathfield Terrace was a four-storey block of flats in a cul-de-sac. Samantha lived in a ground-floor, one-bedroom flat. Cosy might not have lived at the address, but he had his own key and could let himself come and go as he wished.

Cosy found the flat in disarray. Clothes were strewn about, and a trail of blood traversed the tiny property. Samantha lay on her back in the centre of the living room. A cushion had been placed under her bottom, her dressing gown was open, and her bra had been cut in two to expose her breasts. Her arms had been raised above her head, and her face had been covered by clothing and linen. Her abdomen was cut open from the vulva to the throat. There was also a bruise over Samantha's eye, indicating that she had been violently struck before her brutal murder. One of the stab wounds had been delivered with such force it had snapped Samantha's spinal cord. Attempts had been made to dismember her legs, but these had been abandoned, probably because the knife had become too blunted during the earlier dismemberment of the torso.

Police Sergeant Alan Jackman would later describe the scene in vivid detail, "*It was like something out of Dante's Inferno. Her body was cut completely open, the rib cage had been taken out, and the legs had been severed at the knees. The internal organs had been pulled about and repeatedly stabbed. It was beyond belief... In all my years of service, I've never seen anything so dreadful and so horrific. From the state that the body was in, the way she had been attacked and dismembered, this was a crime way, way beyond normality, way out of the ordinary.*"

Samantha's body had been posed in a deliberately sexual manner. This was an important glimpse into the killer's psychology. As Dr Elizabeth Yardley explained, "*He positioned her body on a cushion, and her body was left in the same position as it was when she had sex with her boyfriend. Now, that basically is saying this woman is sexually available. He's trying to create a narrative here. He's trying to say, 'she deserved this,' and that really does tell us about his misogyny.*"

Cosy found Jazmine lying under the duvet in the bedroom. She had been raped and then suffocated. Lividity patination on Jazmine's body indicated that she had been lying on her back for some time after death before her killer had moved her onto her stomach. There was also urine staining on her knickers. This told the police that Jazmine had been sitting upright for at least part of the attack and had wet herself in fear. This clearly indicated to Paul Britton that there had been "*a more complex interaction with the killer who hadn't simply assaulted her as she lay in bed and then smothered her with a pillow.*" The sight of Jazmine lying in bed haunted many of the officers who saw her, "*She had the appearance of being a child asleep,*" Alan Jackman would later say,

"Which was somehow more disturbing than seeing what was left of her mother."

The scene was so horrible, so brutal, it shocked and horrified the officers who had been summoned. Crime scene photographer Carol England was so affected by the crime scene that she resigned from the Metropolitan Police. Another was so psychologically damaged by the scene they were signed off sick with Post Traumatic Stress Disorder, and it was two years before they felt psychologically recovered enough to return to duty.

Detective Constable Graham Cooke was the first officer to arrive at the scene. Seeing red staining on Cosy's hands, he immediately arrested the young man for the double murder. Cosy was immediately taken to Plumstead Police Station to be formally interviewed.

Detective Superintendent Mickey Banks was placed in charge of the investigation. Assessing the scene, he came to the conclusion that Samantha had let the killer into the flat and that they had almost immediately attacked her in the hallway, where there was a large pool of blood. The killer had then dragged Samantha into the living room by her ankles, leaving behind a set of partial footprints made by an Adidas trainer. However, it was later ascertained the killer had gained entry via an unsecured balcony window. As the killer entered, he cut the cord on a set of rattan blinds so that they descended over the window. Possibly hearing an unexpected noise, Samantha went to investigate and found the intruder in the hallway where he had attacked.

Canvassing the residents of Heathfield Terrace, several recalled seeing an old yellow General Post Office van parked on the street in the days before the murders. Nobody recalled having seen the van before, but that week, it was parked in the street several times. Two local dog walkers said they had seen two young men loitering by the van. Both were unkempt and had long hair. Given where the van was parked outside Samantha's flat, the dog walkers assumed the men were friends of Samantha. Enquiries in the wider Plumstead area led the police to a local taxi driver called John Clarke. On Tuesday the 2nd of November, he collected Samantha and Jazmine from Jazmine's nursery. As they drove into Heathfield Terrace, Samantha spotted the van and remarked, "*Oh god, it's the van. I just hope it's not who I think it is.*" Clarke told the police that Samantha seemed "*genuinely alarmed*" at the sight of the van. After speaking with Clarke, finding the van and the two long-haired men became a priority.

Another neighbour reported hearing two men arguing loudly and angrily in Samantha's flat at around 10.30 p.m. the evening before. The neighbour distinctly heard the words, "*Leave it alone,*" being shouted. Another neighbour, Susan Dewar, who lived in Revell Rise, the neighbouring block of flats, had heard a scream at around 3.00 a.m. The scream had been so loud Susan had gotten out of bed and looked out of the window. They saw that the lights were on in Samantha's flat. Susan also told the police that Samantha had seen a peeping tom looking into her bedroom window about a fortnight earlier. Samantha believed this peeping tom had witnessed Samantha and Cosy having sex.

Police also contacted Social Services to see if they had any information about Samantha or if anyone had raised concerns about her relationship with Cosy. There had been one Social Services referral. It had been made by a neighbour concerned by the number of strange men she had seen coming in and out of Samantha's flat at odd hours.

The neighbour's concerns about the strange men coming to the property led the police to ponder if Samantha had been a sex worker. They quickly concluded that she had. They found several discreet adverts that Samantha had placed in local newspapers that advertised "*no strings attached fun liaisons*" in return for "*help with small child's Scholl* (**SIC**) *fees.*"

Unfortunately, the press also found out about the adverts and, repellently, decided that the public wouldn't be as sympathetic or interested in the murder of a sex worker and stopped reporting on the case, "*Just when we needed their help,*" Superintendent Banks angrily lamented, "*What more do the bastards want? Here, you have a lovely mother and her child murdered in the most horrible way, and they just won't take it. It should be all over the place.*"

Dr Elizabeth Yardley believes that the media's treatment of Samantha and Jazmine's murder when compared to the exposure Rachel Nickell's murder received, shines an important light on the media's inherent biases. "*What we have here are judgements about appropriate femininity and appropriate motherhood. So, Rachel was in a secure long-term relationship with her partner, Samantha's daughter's father didn't live with the family. So, all those new right neo-liberal values about what a family should look like are coming out here in the media's choice to emphasise the Nickell case over the Bissett case.*"

Several autopsies had to be carried out. A bloodstain on the couch in the living room indicated that a bloody mass had been placed there. It was suspected that it might have been a part of Samantha's internal organs that the killer had removed and taken away as a trophy. Pathologists Dr Roger Boydell-Smith and Dr Liam Barclay conducted the first autopsy at Greenwich Mortuary. They concluded that two knives had been used on Samantha, one with a blade with a width of 1 centimetre and the other 2.5 centimetres. There was mutilation to the thighs, breasts and genitals. The injuries to the vagina and genitals were so extensive and severe that it was impossible to tell if Samantha had been raped. However, Dr Barclay and Boydell-Smith both concluded that Samantha's murder was undoubtedly sexually motivated. They also concluded that parts of the internal organs had been taken. However, they wanted this to be independently verified, so Dr Ian Hill carried out a second autopsy the following day. His findings as to whether the killer had taken body parts was inconclusive. So, a third autopsy was conducted, this time by Dr Dick Shepherd. He confirmed that a 10cm X 12cm section of the abdominal wall was missing.

The autopsies established the time of death, and this meant that Cosy couldn't possibly have been the killer. He had been at work when Samantha and Jazmine were murdered, with dozens of witnesses to vouch for him. The red stains on his hands were confirmed to be a dye that he used at work. He was released with apologies.

Forensic Officers quickly eliminated almost every single fingerprint found in the flat as belonging to either Samantha, Jazmine or Cosy, all except for one set. These belonged to a local man by the name of Peter Copley. Police went to Copley's house to speak with him. He admitted being friends with Samantha and having visited her at her flat. He stated that on the night of the murder, he had been visiting his ex-wife in Sussex. Suspiciously, he refused to give the police a written statement.

Copley's ex-wife confirmed that he had stayed at her property on the night of the murder, sleeping in a spare room. This led Superintendent Banks to ponder if the alibi was a clever rouse. He had officers time how long it took to drive from Heathfield Terrace to the address in Sussex. The time trials showed that Copley had just about enough time to pretend to go to bed in Sussex, drive to Heathfield Terrace, murder and rape Samantha and Jazmine, clean himself up, and get back to Sussex in time to be found by his ex-wife curled up in the spare room the following morning as if nothing had happened.

Copley had no history of violence, and a quiet word with his ex-wife confirmed there had been no violence within their marriage. He was said to be placid and gentle. Copley appeared to be an ordinary, nice man who had simply had the misfortune to make friends with a woman who had been brutally murdered. The police decided to place Copley on the back burner but keep an eye on him to see if he did anything else suspicious.

It was Detective Sergeant Lionel Barclay who first noted the similarities between Samantha's murder and that of Rachel Nickell. Superintendent Banks agreed with Barclay that the cases could be linked, and he arranged to meet Detective Inspector Keith Peddar at Wimbledon Police Station to discuss both cases. This meeting took place on Wednesday the 10th of November 1993.

During this meeting, Keith Peddar stated categorically that the cases were not connected as they were convinced Colin Stagg had murdered Rachel, and they had him under constant surveillance. Mickey Banks left the meeting feeling frustrated by Peddar's belligerent and blinkard attitude, saying, *"There was no way that you could persuade Keith Peddar or Mick Wickerson, the persons in charge of that enquiry, that anybody but Stagg had done that murder. There was a total blank on it... But they,"* Banks gave a large exasperated sigh, *"But Paul Britton was convinced Stagg was their murderer."*

Keith Peddar told Superintendent Banks how indispensable Paul Britton had been to the Rachel Nickell investigation, and against DS Banks' better judgment, he allowed them to arrange for Paul Britton to look over the Bissett case files and crime scene photographs and come to Thamesmead to speak with DS Banks about his thoughts and conclusions. Paul Britton duly came up with an offender profile that said that Samantha and Jazmine's killer would have the following traits:

- He will have experienced violence in the family home during childhood.

- Will have had a disturbed family life.

- He grew up with a different set of values than most other people, and this may have brought him to the attention of police or Social Services.

- He will feel undervalued.

- He has learned that aggression can solve problems, and it has become a substitute for talking. As a result, he has poor social skills.

- Was not a sadist but gained satisfaction from his interactions with the victim's body.

- He will use contact magazines.

- Normal intelligence.

- He will be single and able to hold down a low-skilled job.

- Have a psychological malfunction that prevents him from sustaining any meaningful relationship.

- He is not seeking notoriety or fame.

- He will have a history of offending against females and cruelty to animals.

- He is a watcher and stalker.

Britton also concluded that two different people had murdered Samantha Bissett and Rachel Nickell. He felt that the killer ignoring the child in one murder whilst the child being an important object of sexual gratification in the other showed a wildly different psychological mindset. He also felt that the killer took much more enjoyment from the post-mortem mutilation during Samantha's murder. In fact, Samantha's killer had enjoyed the mutilating more than the killing itself. This, in Britton's estimation, was completely different to the mindset of Rachel's killer, who had carried out the offence in a quick, angered frenzy.

Whilst Paul Britton's profile was largely ignored by Superintendent Banks, who put little store in such methods, it would later be acknowledged by some of those who worked on the investigation how on the nose this profile was to the psychology of the actual killer.

Police attempted to track down all of the men who had responded to the adverts that Samantha had placed in local papers. Superintendent Banks contacted British Telecom and had them draw up a list of every single telephone call that had come and gone from 1a Heathfield Terrace in the previous twelve months. The names and addresses associated with each number then had to be contacted, and their alibis verified. It was a mammoth undertaking. At the same time, the enquiry team tried to track down the 300 owners of decommissioned General Post Office vans. Then there was a shoe enquiry. The Adidas shoeprint had been estimated to be between a size seven and nine. Small for man. Still, it was a daunting task to ascertain the trainer's exact design and track down where it could have been sold. Then, of course, there was the usual shakedown of local sex offenders and perverts.

After consultation with Adidas, it was concluded that the killer had been wearing Adidas Phantom low or mid-basketball shoes. A special notice was sent out across the Metropolitan Police Force asking all police officers to contact Superintendent Banks if they arrested anyone wearing any such trainers in a size seven to nine. Not long after the notice was sent out, a second search of 1a Heathfield Terrace uncovered a copy of the Daily Mirror TV supplement that had somehow been missed on the initial search. This had an almost pristine footprint upon it. Forensic officers were now able to say with certainty that the killer had size nine feet.

On Thursday the 8th of February 1994, DS Banks and Paul Britton appeared on Crimewatch UK to make an appeal. DS Banks was a little perturbed that the producers wanted most of the focus of the appeal to be on Paul Britton's psychological profile of the killer. DS Banks felt that the profile was evidentially useless and, therefore, a waste of time. However, given the lack of publicity the case had received, he felt that even just a few minutes of prime-time coverage focusing on the psychological profile was better than no publicity at all.

Nick Ross began by stating that the police believed the man responsible would kill again and may have killed before. There was then a reconstruction where Cosy Ellam played himself and reconstructed the moment he entered 1a Heathfield Terrace and found Samantha and Jazmine's bodies. Margaret Morrison was interviewed and said of her daughter, "*She was a loving child, a very caring kind of girl,*" and spoke about her regret at moving back to Scotland after her husband's death and how Samantha's life and death might have been so much different if she remained in Gloucestershire. Home video footage of Samantha and Jazmine walking along a beach was shown.

The appeal mentioned the adverts that Samantha had placed in the local newspapers but played their real purpose down, and Nick Ross told the viewers Samantha was "*hoping to meet friends, she was evidently lonely… It's not clear what she expected, but she was shocked at some of the replies.*"

DS Banks appeared on the show, and he revealed to the public for the first time that Jazmine had been sexually assaulted. He stated that he was making this information public because "*I'm very afraid that this man will murder again, and I'm appealing to people who think they might have an inkling they might know the person might be responsible for these murders, a friend, a relative, perhaps even a wife or a girlfriend. Once they realise what happened to this poor young child, this defenceless young child of four years of age, I'm hoping they will contact us and help us."*

The offender profile was featured, and for the first time in the broadcast, sex work was eluded to, with Ross telling the viewers the killer may have a history of *"hurting prostitutes."* Ross then asked Banks in a very ham-fisted way, *"If he had gone to prostitutes, if he had attacked some sort of woman before, what sort of attack, what would it be she'd recognise in his behaviour?"* DS Banks seemed to look on askance at this peculiarly and offensively phrased question but answered rather plainly and ultimately drew the link between Samantha's adverts and sex work explicitly, *"I think rather than having sex with a prostitute or perhaps someone he's met through a contact magazine he most probably wants to hurt them as opposed to having sex."*

Paul Britton then appeared. He made a very direct appeal to the killer in his very quiet yet authoritative manner, *"I think we know quite well what was going through his mind at the time of the offence, but I would like him to tell me how he got started on the pathway that led him to kill, to harm, Samantha. I would also like him to tell me why it was necessary for him to harm the child as well."*

Two artists' impressions of a man that DS Banks wanted to eliminate from the enquiry were then shown to the viewers. He was a man in his twenties with long hair tied back into a ponytail and an earring in the shape of a cross. It was said that this man had been seen multiple times with Samantha during the summer of 1992 and also bore a striking similarity to the man seen loitering by the decommissioned British Telecom van.

Police officers eagerly sat at a bank of telephones both in BBC Television Centre and back at Plumstead Police Station, waiting for the phones to ring after the appeal. Ultimately, the Crimewatch UK appeal generated no useful leads.

By May 1994, the investigation was at a standstill. All leads that could be chased up had, and all possible suspects had been cleared. Out of desperation, DS Banks asked that the fingerprints found at the crime scene be double-checked. This uncovered a huge blunder. The forensic officers had misidentified several fingerprints. Three fingerprints had wrongly been identified as belonging to Samantha. These had been on the balcony, one on the doorjamb to the bedroom and one on Jazmine's cot. The fingerprints actually belonged to twenty-eight-year-old Robert Clive Napper.

When the incident room got hold of Napper's mugshot, one of the officers looked horrified. Pam Robinson had previously worked on an investigation into four sex attacks carried out by the same man over four years. This person had become known as the Green Chain Rapist. So-called because all of the attacks had taken place along the fifty miles that encompass the Green Chain Walk, a pathway that links three hundred parks, woods, fields and public spaces between the banks of the River Thames and Nunhead Cemetery. Robinson pointed out that Napper was a dead-ringer for the artist's impression of this prolific sex attacker.

Robert Napper was born on Saturday the 25th of February 1967, the exact same day as Samantha Bisset. He was the eldest of four children born to Pauline and Brian Napper. His childhood was marred by domestic violence, with Brian being a brutal father who instilled fear in his children. At Blackfen Primary School, Napper was quiet and withdrawn but, on the whole, well-behaved. However, he was once caught stealing from fellow pupils and was severely disciplined for the offence. Napper was bullied terribly throughout his schooling both at Blackfen Primary and later at Abbey Wood Comprehensive, and it was later said by other pupils that Napper was "despised" by the other children. As a result of the bullying, Napper regularly truanted from school.

When Napper was twelve, he was taken away for the weekend on a camping trip arranged by a family friend. Whilst on the trip, Napper was sexually assaulted. Upon his return from the trip, Napper immediately told his mother, and the man who carried out the sexual assault was ultimately arrested, convicted and sent to prison. However, the sexual assault haunted young Napper, and it was said that his personality completely changed after the event.

As Napper was bullied at school, so he became a bully towards his siblings. His actions towards them weren't just nasty and cruel but dangerous. He once fired an airgun into his brother's face, seriously hurting him. Napper's sister became aware that her older brother was spying on her when she took baths and got changed out of her clothes. Over time, Napper's sister developed a real fear of her older brother.

In 1976, Napper and his siblings were temporarily placed into local authority care. It was identified that Napper had been seriously traumatised by the domestic abuse he had witnessed, and he was treated at Maudsley Psychiatric Hospital until the age of sixteen. Throughout his life, Napper displayed symptoms of serious mental health problems. He was known to talk and argue with himself regularly, and several people saw him on several occasions shouting abuse into the sky. He suffered from severe delusions. He also displayed constant paranoia and had a belief that he was being spied on. In later life, this led to him frequently changing addresses.

In 1982, Napper left Abbey Wood Comprehensive after failing to achieve his secondary qualifications. He subsequently obtained various types of employment in areas of work as varied as the catering trade, a barman, and even an electrician's mate. His periods of employment were initially short-lived. He had trouble fitting in wherever he went and was invariably fired after only a few short weeks. In 1989, Napper found one job he could stick it out at. He was employed by Serco cataloguing a multitude of long-forgotten storerooms as the Ministry of Defence decommissioned the Royal Woolwich Arsenal. It was a solitary job that didn't bring Napper into contact with many other people, so it suited him. Those staff members who did encounter Napper thought he was 'weird', and it was said that the female staff were especially wary of him. Napper worked at Woolwich Arsenal from 1989 to 1992, when the site was finally closed, and he was made redundant.

In early 1992, Napper attempted to shoot a woman he had been stalking. Her house boarded Plumstead Common, where Napper carried out the majority of his offences. The woman had been in her kitchen when the window exploded.

Mercifully unhurt in the incident, the woman subsequently found a .22 bullet embedded in her kitchen wall. Some time later, on Friday the 19th of February 1993, two children playing in the woods on Winns Common came across a half-buried Happy Shopper biscuit tin that contained a .22 Mauser handgun. The boys told their parents, who reported the find to the police. At the time, the police did not connect the gun to the earlier shooting, and neither event was connected to Robert Napper. That is until his subsequent arrest for murder when his palm print was found to be a match for one found on the biscuit tin lid.

In February 1994, Napper obtained employment with Glyndon Plastics. Here, Napper's timekeeping was said to be abysmal, and he had a habit of missing shifts without telephoning in to explain why. He had to be given an official warning for these behaviours, which he seemed to take exception to. Once again, Napper didn't fit in with the other staff members, and there were several complaints from female staff that he acted inappropriately and generally creeped them out.

As for his official criminal history, Napper first came to the police's attention in August 1986, when he was given a 12-month Conditional Discharge for Possession Of An Offensive Weapon. The weapon in question had been a loaded air rifle. In December 1992, he received eight weeks imprisonment for Possession Of a Firearm and Ammunition Without Certification. His arrest for this offence arose from a bizarre and worrying set of circumstances. Staff at Jetsam Press in Plumstead became concerned when Napper asked them to make up 50 sheets of A4 letterheaded paper using the Metropolitan Police Logo and his contact details at the bottom of the page instead of a legitimate police station. Napper was subsequently arrested for impersonating a police officer. The police searched Nappers' home address and found a .22 Erma pistol, 200 rounds of ammunition, a crossbow and a listening device. Before his sentencing, a psychological report was ordered, which concluded that Napper was *"without doubt an immediate threat to himself and the public."*

Aside from these two convictions, Napper had been suspected of being a local peeping tom. Suspicion fell on Napper after he was seen standing on a wall peering into the home of a single blonde female who lived on Rutherglen Road, Plumstead. A neighbour saw Napper and chased him off. The police took the neighbour on a drive around the local neighbourhood, and they found Napper loitering suspiciously by some garages. The neighbour identified Napper immediately as the peeping tom. At the time, one of the officers made a note in his notebook about Napper, *"Subject strange, abnormal, should be considered a possible rapist, indecency type suspect."* Despite these concerns, the local bobbies only gave Napper a strongly worded verbal warning about his voyeuristic behaviours but took no further action against him.

There was also a note on his official file that in 1989, Napper's mother had reported to Plumstead Police that Napper had confessed to raping a woman on Plumstead Common. At the time, the police checked their records and found no reported offences matching the details, so they decided to take no further action. In fact, the confession coincided with the first Green Chain Rape attack. The rapist had broken into a house that backed onto Winns Common and raped a woman in one of the upstairs bedrooms whilst her children breakfasted downstairs. The rape had, in fact, been reported to the police and had received much publicity due to the brutality of the attack. The confusion had arisen due to Winns Common and Plumstead Common effectively being one large park with a road dividing them, and the locals colloquially referred to the area as a whole as Plumstead Common.

Shortly after the first Green Chain Rape attack, Napper took an overdose of paracetamol and antipsychotic drugs, and on Wednesday the 6th of September 1989, he was admitted into Brook Hospital for treatment. The suicide attempt was put down as another complication of Napper's complex mental health issues. No one linked the suicide attempt to the recent much-publicised rape. Upon being discharged, Napper returned to the family home. A few days later, he packed up all his belongings and moved out, and he never spoke to his mother or siblings again.

Napper was immediately placed under police surveillance. He lived just half a mile away from 1a Heathfield Terrace in a bedsit at 135 Plumstead High Street. DS Banks also consulted Detective Superintendent Steven Landeryou and Detective Inspector John Pearse, who had been in charge of Operation Eccleston, the investigation into the Green Chain Rapist. Landeryou and Pearse informed Banks that Napper had briefly been considered a suspect in the rapes but had been ruled out as the rapist was thought to be 5 foot 7 or 8 inches in height, and Napper was 6 foot 1 inches. Banks asked if Napper had been ruled out using DNA, and Landeryou and Pearse confirmed that Napper had not. It was explained that Napper had become a possible person of interest as Operation Eccleston was being wound down. Napper had been asked to come in and provide a sample of DNA but refused, and the senior officers had chosen not to follow this up due to the height discrepancy.

It was decided to arrest Napper on Friday the 27th of May 1994. Even with the twenty-four-hour surveillance, the police had been unable to ascertain which bedsit Napper lived in, and with his history of weapons offences, it was decided to arrest him as he made his way to work rather than be caught in closed quarters with a desperate man and a weapon. However, Napper had been sacked the previous day due to his poor timekeeping, and police were forced to ask neighbours which bedsit he lived in and break the door to his room down to make the arrest. Napper was arrested without any trouble, and his only comment was to state that he didn't know who Samantha or Jazmine were, and that he had never been to 1a Heathfield Terrace. Obviously, the police knew this to be a lie, thanks to the fingerprint evidence.

Napper was found to be living in a windowless room with no bed, just a dirty old mattress on the floor with a pile of clothes next to it. A search of the property uncovered an empty box for a pair of size 9 Adidas Phantom low-basketball shoes and the receipt given to Napper when he had bought them. The shoes were now missing. They also recovered a receipt for a 'Special Operations Government' hunting knife bought for £62.45 from a mail-order company. Like the shoes, the knife was now missing. The search also uncovered an A-to-Z with annotations written by Napper on the pages that covered the Green Chain Walk, Wimbledon Common, and Heathfield Terrace. Strange notes were written on the pages, such as '*cling film on the legs.*' Along with the A-to-Z were several hand-drawn maps. These highlighted places where Napper could hide and spy on victims, such as woodlands, storm drains, old Second World War bomb shelters and foxholes. Something that became of paramount significance later was a padlocked red metal toolbox. There was also a photocopied page from a book called 'The Dragon's Touch', which detailed how to decapitate someone.

Taken to Bexleyheath Police Station, Paul Britton was on hand to give forensic psychological advice to the interviewing police officers. Due to Napper's history of mental health issues, he was also assigned an appropriate adult who was a clinical psychologist from Maudsley Psychiatric Hospital. A sample of Napper's blood was immediately taken and sent for urgent analysis.

The police interview was a very stop-start affair. Every time the police seemed to box Napper into a corner or ask him a difficult question, Napper would ask for a private consultation with his solicitor. The longest period of sustained questioning lasted just twenty-seven minutes. *"His interview was stone cold,"* DS Banks would later say, *"He seemed as if he was looking down on us. That he knew something we didn't know, and he seemed to my mind that he was sort of 'you're never going find out I'm who I am; I'm better than you.' In his own mind, he was laughing at us."*

Despite the difficulties of the police interview, the police felt they had enough circumstantial evidence to charge Napper with Samantha and Jazmine's murders. On Sunday the 29th of May 1994, Napper was taken from his cell and was formally charged with double murder. Napper made no response to the charge.

Not long after charging Napper with the double murder, DNA tests proved beyond any doubt that Napper was the Green Chain Rapist. DNA identification was in its relative infancy as a forensic tool; the wider public was yet to have a full understanding of how it could pinpoint an offender with 100% accuracy, and so to shore up the case against Napper even further, Napper was placed in several identity parades. Only one of the Green Chain Rape victims failed to identify Napper as being their attacker, and this was because, on that occasion, Napper had worn a mask.

Given what was now known about Robert Napper and his crimes, DS Banks once again contacted the officers investigating the murder of Rachel Nickell and mooted that Napper was a good suspect. Once again, DS Banks was given the brush-off. Several years later, retired Detective Sergeant Alan Jackaman would suggest that this was most likely because the team investigating Rachel's murder didn't want a group of outsiders who hadn't investigated Rachel's murder getting the credit for solving the case. Instead, the Rachel Nickell team decided to cling to the deluded idea that Colin Stagg was still their man despite the collapse of his trial. The remnants of the Nickell investigation team kept Stagg under constant surveillance for a further twelve months after the trial had ended.

When consulted for advice, Paul Britton altered his original opinion that there were two separate killers. On reflection, Britton now also agreed that Napper was a good suspect for Rachel's murderer. He pointed out that the chances of two sexually motivated psychotic killers operating in such a small geographical area at the same time were infinitesimally small. DS Banks tried to escalate the matter but was instructed by his superiors to concentrate on getting Napper convicted for the murder of Samantha and Jazmine.

Meanwhile, between February and September 1995, Napper was assessed by five separate psychologists and psychiatrists. These interviews exposed the depths of Napper's mental illness. He told the psychiatrists that he was the only one who had realised that a government experiment had doubled the length of the years 1973, 1975, 1977, 1979 and 1980. Each of these years had been 730 days long, and only he had seemed to notice. Napper believed that this experience had ruined his childhood. He told another psychiatrist that he'd had a falling out with the queen, whom he'd met in *"hush-hush circumstances"* because he had been unable to attend two charity events she had personally invited him to. He'd won the Nobel Peace Prize three times by the time he was ten years old. He claimed to have been the victim of a poisoning plot by his former landlady and that she used to burn his testicles with a lighter when he was sleeping. That Irish paramilitaries had kneecapped him. They'd also sent him an incendiary device through the post, which had blown off his fingers. When it was pointed out that he still had all his digits, Napper claimed that his father had glued them back on for him. He claimed he was a decorated war hero who had served in the Angolan Civil War. He was secretly a millionaire, but a Roman Catholic sect called The Roman Corinthian Diddycoys was plotting to steal his fortune. He'd made his fortune by penning the screenplays for the Star Wars trilogy of movies, but George Lucas had taken the credit. Nevertheless, George was still good enough to send Napper regular royalty cheques, which had made him richer than Midas. Because of his achievements, he'd been given a much-coveted entry in Who's Who. Oh, and he was also gifted with the preternatural ability of telepathy.

Each psychiatrist agreed that Napper manifested obsessional thoughts and noted that he constantly talked about himself in the third person. They also noted that he viewed women not as people but as objects that were unobtainable to him. He was diagnosed variously as suffering from paranoid schizophrenia, characterised by paranoia, grandiosity and hallucinatory experiences, Asperger's syndrome, and a schizoid personality. One psychiatrist even went so far as to say that Napper only had "*a tenuous link with reality.*" Several of the psychiatrists even believed that Napper was not fit to plead at his coming trial. As a result of these assessments, Napper was transferred to Broadmoor Secure Hospital under Section 48 of the Mental Health Act 1983.

Shortly before the trial was due to commence, Margaret Morrison died. Her husband, Jack, said that she had never fully recovered from the brutal deaths of her only child and grandchild. The death was said to greatly affect the investigative team, who were still working on making the case against Robert Napper as watertight as possible for the trial. The death galvanised them and made them determined to secure a conviction in tribute for Margaret.

Robert Napper's trial commenced at the Old Bailey before Mr Justice Hooper on Monday the 4th of September 1995. Mr Justice Hooper was educated at Sherborne School, one of Britain's oldest public schools, before going on to read law at Trinity Hall, Cambridge. He was called to the bar in 1965 and touched silk in 1987. He'd only recently been awarded his High Court judgeship after serving as a recorder since 1976, and the Napper case was his first big trial.

Nigel Sweeney QC prosecuted, assisted by junior counsel David Spens. Bizarrely, William Clegg QC, fresh from his victory in the Colin Stagg trial, had been appointed as Napper's defence barrister.

Nigel Sweeney was a legal big hitter. He specialised in prosecuting high-profile, complicated cases such as the IRA Brighton Bombers and was the man who secured the controversial conviction of the alleged murderer Michael Stone[xvii]. He had read law at the University of Nottingham and was called to the bar in 1976. Sweeney went on to become a High Court Judge and presided at the trial of celebrity sex offender Rolf Harris and disgraced MPs Chris Huhne and Denis McShane.

The first order of business was for the jury to decide if Napper was fit to plead. The evidence from the various psychiatrists and psychologists was laid before the jury, and they decided that Napper was mentally fit and well enough to understand the legal proceedings and place his plea. Then there came a very large surprise: after protesting his innocence since the day of his arrest, William Clegg told the Court that Napper was willing to plead Guilty to the lesser charge of Manslaughter on the grounds of diminished responsibility as outlined under the Mental Health Act 1957. The prosecution, well aware of Napper's complex mental health issues, accepted the plea. *"I was satisfied with that,"* DS Banks would later say when asked about Napper pleading to a lesser charge, "*I mean, I believe he was diminished. He wasn't so mad that he didn't know what he was doing; he knew what he was doing, but there was something totally wrong with him.*"

Due to the plea that the prosecution had accepted, Napper could not be sentenced to the term of life imprisonment that a murderer would usually receive. Instead, he was sentenced to a Restriction Order under Section 41 of the Mental Health Act 1983. This effectively meant that Napper would be detained indefinitely at Broadmoor High Secure Hospital. His discharge from the hospital could only be authorised by the Home Secretary[xviii].

In early 1996, Detective Superintendent Peter Charnley was set the task of seeing if he could salvage anything from the investigation into Rachel Nickell's murder. One of his first tasks was to speak with Detective Superintendent Banks about the possibility that Robert Napper had been Rachel's killer. Banks told Charnley that he firmly believed Napper was the man responsible for Rachel's murder and that this should be the focus of his investigation. So, it was decided that Napper should be interviewed formally about Rachel's murder. The Metropolitan Police were still smarting over the collapse of the Colin Stagg trial and officially still maintaining that they were not looking for anyone else in connection to the murder. So, to save face, it was decided that one of the officers who had worked on the Samantha and Jazmine Bisset investigation should be sent to interview Napper under the guise of a post-conviction interview.

Napper refused to admit anything. He said he had been at work on the day of Rachel's murder. Charnley tried to check this alibi but discovered that Serco had destroyed Napper's work records. On the face of it, it appeared to be an investigative dead end. Ultimately, DS Charnley toed the party line, and in his final report to the top brass at Scotland Yard, he concluded that Colin Stagg had murdered Rachel.

Colin Stagg was finally completely exonerated in 2004. A cold case review of several unsolved cases sent items related to Rachel's murder off for forensic testing, and for the first time, a DNA profile was retrieved from the semen staining on the jogging bottoms. However, the DNA sample recovered was considered not viable enough to make any comparisons with any suspects. Not happy with this finding, the cold case review team sent the DNA to a different lab that was using more up-to-date cutting-edge technology. They were able to identify the DNA found on Rachel's jogging bottoms and put a name to the killer. It was convicted double murderer Robert Clive Napper.

Wanting to be 100% certain of a conviction, the case was handed over to the Major Investigation Team. They went back over Napper's alibi for the day of Rachel's murder. Rather than just speaking to representatives of Serco, they actually interviewed other employees. Napper's boss had the foresight to keep his year planner from 1992. This showed that on Thursday the 15th of July 1992, Robert Napper had the day off. Napper had been lying all along.

The case against Napper was strengthened when the clothes he had been wearing when he was arrested for Samantha and Jazmine's murder were removed from storage and sent for testing. The MIT team were interested in Napper's shoes. These were sent for analysis to compare them with the plaster cast of the footprints found at the side of the stream where one of the witnesses in the Nickell case had seen a suspect male cleaning his hands. They matched perfectly.

Then, there was that red metal toolbox discovered at Napper's flat. At the time of Napper's arrest, no significance had been given to this toolbox. However, when Alex Nickell was examined after Rachel's murder, forensic officers discovered minute traces of red metal paint in his hair. For years, this paint and how it came to be in Alex's hair had flummoxed the police. However, when these flakes of paint were compared to the paint on the red metal toolbox, they were found to be chemically identical. It seemed, somehow, the paint had transferred from the toolbox onto Robert Napper and from Napper onto little baby Alex.

Armed with the new evidence, Napper was interviewed under caution at Broadmoor Hospital. He made no comment to all questions, but his solicitor had prepared a statement in which he simply retread his original story. He had been at work on the day of Rachel's murder and had no information that could help the police. Knowing full well that this was a lie, Napper was charged with Rachel's murder.

Robert Napper's trial for the murder of Rachell Nickell commenced at the Old Bailey on Thursday, the 18th of December 2008, before Mr Justice Griffiths-Williams. Victor Temple QC prosecuted, and David Fisher QC stood for the defence. It was a very perfunctory affair that was over in a matter of minutes. Robert Napper appeared only via video link. Napper pled guilty to manslaughter on the grounds of diminished responsibility. The prosecution accepted the plea. Mr Justice Griffiths-Williams informed Napper that he would continue to be held indefinitely at Broadmoor Secure Hospital, and the proceedings were concluded. It was a perfunctory and anti-climactic end to one of the most controversial and complicated murder investigations in British criminal history.

In the wake of Napper's conviction, Colin Stagg was issued widely publicised apologies from the Metropolitan Police and Crown Prosecution Service. He was ultimately awarded £706,000 compensation for his wrongful prosecution. He would later tell the press that he had forgiven the investigating officers for their having persecuted him but said he could never forgive Paul Britton for masterminding Operation Edzell and playing so coldly and calculatingly with his emotions. However, Stagg also lamented that the conviction of Robert Napper for Rachel's murder did not receive as wide publicity as his own trial. He stated that he still met people who did not know that Rachel's killer had been caught and still believed him to be the guilty party.

A review by the Independent Police Complaints Commission was damning of both the investigation into the murder of Rachel Nickell and the Green Chain Rape Investigation. They concluded that Napper should have been investigated more thoroughly when his mother came to the police with the allegations of rape in 1989. That Robert Napper should never have been ruled out of that investigation as a suspect based on his height alone. Most damningly, they concluded that if the police had done their job properly during the Green Chain Rape investigation, Rachel, Samantha, and Jazmine would never have been murdered. As a result of these conclusions, Commander Simon Foy of Scotland Yard issued an apology to the families of Rachel, Samantha and Jazmine.

All of the key officers involved in the Green Chain Rape investigation and the Rachel Nickell investigation had long retired by the time the Independent Police Complaints Commission report was published, and no one faced disciplinary proceedings for their failures. Rachel's partner, André Anscombe, told the press that despite the mistakes made during the investigation, the family felt that the police never gave "*anything less than the best.*"

Lizzie James took early retirement from the Metropolitan Police, and then she sued them for the psychological damage she alleges was caused by Operation Edzell. She also claimed that being part of the uncover operation irreparably damaged her career. She settled out of court and received £125,000 in compensation. By comparison, Alex Nickell was awarded just £22,000 compensation by the Criminal Injuries Compensation Authority for having witnessed the brutal murder of his mother.

In 2002, Paul Britton faced a misconduct hearing brought against him by the British Psychological Society. The misconduct hearing came about after a complaint made by Colin Stagg about Britton's conduct during Operation Edzell. The BPS had taken four years to investigate the complaint before starting the formal hearings. Like Colin Stagg's trial, the misconduct hearing collapsed due to a lack of evidence. Paul Britton was allowed to keep his accreditation from the BPS and continue practising forensic psychology in the public sector. Nevertheless, Mr Britton said that the way the BPS had treated him had taken a terrible toll on his physical and mental health.

The use of Psychological Profiling by British law enforcement agencies was effectively put to an end after the collapse of the Colin Stagg trial. In the wake of the trials collapse, The Police Review, a weekly professional publication for serving police officers, ran a screaming headline that simply read '*A Science Discredited*'. The Guardian similarly ran an article that had the headline '*Psychological Profiling Worse Than Useless*' and proclaimed, "*Profiling of killers has no real-world value, wastes police time and risks bringing the profession into disrepute.*" The Home Office continues to maintain a register of experts who can provide psychological profiles. However, the Home Office's official stance is that psychological profiles are no longer used for criminal investigations.

Police continue to investigate Robert Napper's crimes. They now believed he may have committed as many as 86 rapes and 106 sexual assaults between 1988 and 1994.

You're Not A Serial Killer, Right?: Robin West, Joanne Brown and Sarah Butler

Our next case is a stark and horrid reminder that justice is not truly blind. It makes painfully clear that even in this day and age, the colour of a victim's skin can influence whether justice is served. The victims in this next shocking tale were all vulnerable black women, chosen by a cold and calculating killer for this very reason, as he knew that the police wouldn't put as much effort into solving their deaths as they might if the victim had been a white person. Even typing those words turns my stomach, yet there we are. This case will undoubtedly infuriate you as you read it, leaving you shocked and saddened.

Robin West was just nineteen. She was the daughter of Leroy and Anita West. She had a good, if strict, upbringing. Her father was a police officer and pastor at the local church, so there were firm rules and boundaries in Robin's life. When Leroy and Anita divorced, Robin lived with Anita but had regular contact with Leroy. She regularly attended church, where she was a star of the choir. Throughout her life, Robin suffered from mental health issues. Troubled since childhood, she'd spent time at the Wordsworth Academy, a rehabilitation centre for children with behavioural and mental health issues. Here, Robin was subject to a brutal regime, which involved physical assaults from staff, and other residents were brave enough to report sexual abuse.

Robin's family couldn't understand why Robin seemed to be hellbent on rebelling against her parent's rules and wishes when her two siblings happily lived within the strict boundaries set. When Robin's behavioural and mental health issues grew more problematic, her parents and loved ones struggled to cope with the troubled teen. As soon as she could, Robin left home in an act of further rebellion. Robin seemed almost spitefully to cut her family off. Not contacting her parents or siblings for months at a time. This isolation compounded her mental health problems. Moving from Chester, Pennsylvania, to Union Township, New Jersey, meant Robin no longer had any support networks in place in her life. Robin ended up homeless and living temporarily at the Garden State Motor Lodge. She was lonely and isolated. With no source of income and no familial help to fall back on, Robin turned to exotic dancing and then to prostitution to support herself.

At a little after 11.00 p.m. on Wednesday the 31st of August 2016, Robin was propositioned by a curb crawler on Nye Avenue on Newark's south side. The curb crawler was a young black man driving a silver BMW Sudan. Robin was with a friend called Brunisha Patterson, and Brunisha would later say that the young man was good-looking and charming and appeared entirely harmless. Robin agreed to do business with the man and got in his car. As the car drove off, Brunisha Patterson noted down the number plate of the car on her mobile phone. This was the last time Robin was seen alive.

In the early hours of Thursday the 1st of September 2016, a fire was reported at an abandoned house on Lakeside Avenue in Orange, New Jersey. When the fire was extinguished, Robin's body was discovered. A seventeen-year veteran of the New Jersey Fire Department told the press it was the most destructed body he had ever seen. Duct tape had been wrapped around Robin's head, and she had been raped and strangled with an item of her own clothing. Due to the severity of the burns, it took the police two weeks to identify Robin's body, and even then, this was only possible with reference to her dental records.

When police established the identity of the burnt corpse, it didn't take them long to track down Robin's known associates. The police came and spoke to Brunisha Patterson. Brunisha gave the police the registration details of the car Robin had last been seen getting into. The car was registered to a twenty-year-old local man by the name of Khalil Wheeler-Weaver. New Jersey Police say they spoke with Wheeler-Weaver as part of their investigation. However, the officers sent to speak with the young man were satisfied with the account he gave of himself. Given what we now know about what subsequently transpired, I find this explanation problematic and worrying. The New Jersey Police Department quickly shelved the investigation into Robin West's murder.

Joanne Brown was thirty-three and homeless. She was originally from Augusta, Maine, but moved to Newark when she was five. Like Robin West, Joanne had struggled with her mental health. She had a dual diagnosis of bipolar disorder and schizophrenia. There is a lot of stigma around such serious mental health conditions, none more so than around schizophrenia. It is an entirely treatable illness, and those who have the condition can live entirely normal lives unaffected by symptoms if they regularly take their medication and live as structured a life as possible. Unfortunately, Joanne didn't live a structured or ordered life and failed to take her medication with any great regularity. Her mental health became compounded by her falling into drug misuse. Then, like Robin West, Joanne had taken to supporting herself and her addiction via exotic dancing, and from this, she progressed to prostitution.

Joanne was last seen alive at 1.15 p.m. on Saturday the 22nd of October 2016. Joanne was working Springfield Avenue in Newark's redlight districts when a curb crawler driving a silver BMW Sedan pulled up alongside her. The driver was a good-looking young black man. Joanne got into the car alongside the driver and was not seen alive again. Whilst in the car with the client, she asked if she could use his phone to telephone a friend. The client obligingly let Joanne use his mobile phone to make the call. A little later that day, Joanne's friend received a second call from the same number. This time, it wasn't Joanne calling. There was a man on the other end of the line heavily breathing. This went on for several seconds. Then, the caller disconnected the call without saying anything.

On Monday the 5th of December 2015, a work crew found Joanne's body in another abandoned house on Highland Avenue, Orange. Joanne had been raped. Her eyes and mouth had been covered with duct tape, and her own jacket had been used to strangle her to death.

Police spoke to the friend who had received the strange telephone call on the day Joanne had disappeared. The police said that there was little they could do with just a telephone number. They claim that in an act of supreme incompetence, they made no effort to find out who the telephone number was registered to. Just like the investigation into Robin West's murder, the investigation into Joanne Brown's murder was also shelved.

Thirty-three-year-old Tiffany Taylor was another extremely vulnerable woman. She had grown up in Jersey before attending Florida State University, where she read music and psychology. After graduating, she moved back to Jersey, where she became a professional dancer. When she struggled to make ends meet in her chosen profession, in desperation, she turned to sex work. By April 2016, Tiffany was at a low ebb. She found herself homeless, living out of her car and pregnant. Then, she was introduced by a mutual friend to a twenty-year-old local man named Khalil Wheeler-Weaver. They became friends. They started hanging out together and shared a love of video games, which they would sit and play for hours. Then Wheeler-Weaver began to show a romantic interest in Tiffany. From a good family, Wheeler-Weaver was respectable, in full-time employment that paid well and had positive aspirations for the future. He was the type of respectable, clean-cut young man Tiffany's parents had always wanted her to end up with.

Over the course of a week, Wheeler-Weaver love-bombed Tiffany. It was like he was obsessed with her. He was constantly sending her text message after text message of increasing flirtatiousness. For a woman who was thirteen years older than him, on her uppers and at a low ebb, the attention from the attractive young man was flattering. However, she was still reluctant to turn the friendship into something romantic. Eventually, Wheeler-Weaver sweetened the deal by offering to pay for Tiffany to have sex with him.

Tiffany drove to Wheeler-Weaver's apartment. She went in, and Wheeler-Weaver paid her the money for the sex upfront. Tiffany immediately got a bad vibe from Wheeler-Weaver. She felt that something wasn't right. She was feeling increasingly uncomfortable by their interaction. When Wheeler-

Weaver began to make the expected sexual advances, Tiffany felt instinctively that she was in danger. Tiffany made an excuse to leave, telling Wheeler-Weaver that she had left her condoms in the car. She went back to the car, got in, and drove home.

By November 2016, Tiffany was starting to get back on her feet. She had secured employment as a cleaner for the Ritz Motel on Highway One. She had also been given a room by the management. Therefore, Tiffany was a little confused when she began receiving sexually suggestive text messages from a number she did not recognise. It was Khalil Wheeler-Weaver. Once again, he sent message after message begging Tiffany to meet up with him. Remembering their last uncomfortable interaction, Tiffany refused. Once again, Wheeler-Weaver offered to pay for Tiffany's company. Still desperately in need of money, Tiffany agreed.

On Tuesday the 15th of November 2016, Tiffany met Wheeler-Weaver at the Ritz Motel, which was based in Elizabeth, New Jersey. They both got in Wheeler-Weaver's silver BMW Sudan car and set off to look for a quiet location where they could have sex. After driving for a little while, Wheeler-Weaver pulled over, telling Tiffany that he needed to urinate. *"That was the last thing I remember,"* Tiffany would later say, *"Then I woke up in the back seat, and I was being choked out and raped from behind ... and then he strangled me more ... and I passed out."*

Wheeler-Weaver had bashed Tiffany over the head, knocking her into unconsciousness. After he had finished raping Tiffany, Wheeler-Weaver handcuffed her and placed duct tape around her eyes. Wheeler-Weaver had no idea that Tiffany was double-jointed, allowing her to slip her hands out of the handcuffs.

Despite the traumatic experience Tiffany was going through, she somehow kept her wits about her. She told Wheeler-Weaver that she had left her mobile phone at the motel, and this had incriminating messages on it that would lead the police directly to Wheeler-Weaver if she were to disappear. The ruse worked, and Wheeler-Weaver agreed to take Tiffany back to the motel so that she could collect the mobile phone and hand it over. Tiffany couldn't believe her luck that Wheeler-Weaver had agreed to take her back to a place of safety. She would later say, "*I don't understand some of the stupid things he did. It's like he wanted to get caught.*"

When they arrived at the motel, Tiffany ran into the motel room and refused to come back out. Wheeler-Weaver banged angrily on the door to the room and began shouting violent threats through the door. When this attracted unwanted attention, he fled. "*I wasn't planning on dying that day,*" Tiffany would later say, "*My every thought was to get away.*"

Tiffany telephoned the New Jersey Police Department and reported the kidnapping, rape, and attempted murder. Shockingly, the police didn't believe Tiffany. She was a homeless former sex worker, and what was more, she was black. The man she was accusing had no criminal convictions and came from a respected family with several connections to the local police department. Tiffany was accusing the stepson of a respected detective, and his uncle was likewise a long-serving, recently retired police detective. Indeed, it was expected that Khalil Wheeler-Weaver would likewise join the police force as soon as he was old enough. He was at that time gaining experience working as a security guard for a company called Sterling Securities. Sterling Securities was owned by two former police officers who were friends with Wheeler-Weaver's stepfather and uncle. The New Jersey Police Department took no further action against Khalil Wheeler-Weaver.

The New Jersey Police's incompetence, combined with their misogynistic and racist attitudes, allowed Khalil Wheeler-Weaver to kill again. Sarah Butler was just twenty years old and studying dance at New Jersey City University. At the time of her disappearance, she was visiting home for Thanksgiving. While visiting her family, Sarah began using the dating app Tagged to look for casual hookups. She was unlucky enough to encounter Khalil Wheeler-Weaver. They began to send each other flirty messages. After a failed date where Sarah got cold feet and stood him up, Wheeler-Weaver offered Sarah $500 to meet up with him. Just before meeting Wheeler-Weaver on Tuesday the 22nd of November 2016, Sarah sent him a message that said, *"You're not a serial killer, right? Lmao."*

When Sarah went missing, her family and friends were frantic. Their anxiety increased when the mini-van Sarah had been driving was found abandoned in Orange with one of her hair extensions ripped out and discarded on the floor of the vehicle. Desperately wanting to help, one of Sarah's friends informed the family that Sarah had been using the dating app Tagged to meet up with new people. Sarah's sister, Aliyah Butler, was able to log on to Sarah's profile and found the messages arranging a date with Wheeler-Weaver for the night she disappeared. Aliyah then set up a fake profile and began to message Wheeler-Weaver in a catfishing operation. She lured Wheeler-Weaver to the Panera Bread fast-food restaurant next to Glenfield Park, and when he arrived, Aliyah telephoned the police and told them her suspicions that he had murdered her sister.

Once again, the New Jersey Police reacted with scepticism and let Wheeler-Weaver go. However, on Thursday the 1st of December 2016, Sarah's body was found dumped at Eagle Rock Reservation nature reserve. It had half-heartedly been covered over with some rocks and leaves. Once again, the Butler family reiterated their suspicions about Khalil Wheeler-Weaver. This time, the New Jersey Police couldn't ignore the allegations against the favourite son of the prominent law enforcement family, and, perhaps a little reluctantly, they began to look a little closer at Khalil Wheeler-Weaver. To their surprise, using his mobile phone data and internet searches, the police were able to place Khalil Wheeler-Weaver directly at the scene of Sarah's murder.

On Tuesday the 6th of December 2016, Wheeler-Weaver was arrested at his home for the murder of Sarah Butler. As they explored the mobile phone data further, the police were able to track Wheeler-Weaver's movements over the previous months and also place him at the scenes of Robin West and Joanne Brown's murders. It also showed that he had returned to the scenes of his crimes when the bodies were discovered, and crowds had formed to ogle the police at work. There was also a record on the phone of the telephone call made by Joanne Brown to her friend on the day she disappeared, and a record of the heavy breathing call the friend had received later that same day.

Khalil Wheeler-Weaver was a quiet, lonely individual. Born on Saturday the 20th of April 1996, he grew up in the Seven Oaks district of Newark. He had been seen as a bit of a geek in school. He didn't do sports. He concentrated on academic activities, so he'd never been truly popular. He worked as a security guard at a local hotel and a supermarket, and in his spare time, he liked to DJ and had, in fact, secured a few gigs at local parties. The few friends he had all said that he was extremely quiet and hardly ever spoke, but when he did, he was very amusing.

There were none of the usual indicators one would expect to see in a serial killer's upbringing or past behaviours: no childhood traumas, no childhood abuse, no head injuries, no allegations of bullying, criminality or cruelty. No one had ever thought that this quiet, studious, unassuming young man was the least bit dangerous, let alone a devious, sexual deviant and sadistic killer. A family friend would later say, *"Surprised is a loose word. Surprised, I'm flabbergasted beyond belief."*

Khalil Wheeler-Weaver's trial commenced on Friday the 25th of October 2019, at Newark State Courthouse before Judge Mark Ali. Assistant District Attorneys Carolyn Murray and Adam Wells conducted the prosecution. Although little physical evidence linked Wheeler-Weaver to the crimes, the prosecutors had a strong but mainly circumstantial case. Wheeler-Weaver could be linked to each of the victims via the messages he had sent them in the weeks leading up to their deaths, and his mobile phone data placed him at the scenes of the crimes. He'd made internet searches for *'What chemical could you put on a rag and hold on a person's face to induce sleep'* and *'How to make homemade poisons to murder humans.'* Just two hours before messaging Sarah Butler to arrange their fatal encounter, Wheeler-Weaver had googled various date rape drugs. He lived just a short two-minute drive from the abandoned house where Joanne Brown had been murdered. The mini-van Sarah Butler had been driving the night she disappeared had been abandoned just six blocks from his house. There was one final piece of evidence that was far from circumstantial. It put the final damning cherry on the cake. Khalil Wheeler-Weaver's DNA matched DNA found on Robin West's body.

The prosecution stated that Wheeler-Weaver targeted the women because they were black and vulnerable, and as such, he knew the police wouldn't put as much effort into solving their murders, *"They were viewed as somehow less than human, less valuable,"* Adam Wells told the jury.

Wheeler-Weaver's attorney, Shevelle McPherson, stated that the case against her client was "*very circumstantial.*" In fact, Wheeler-Weaver didn't deny that he had met every single one of the victims and that he had sexual encounters with each one of them. Wheeler-Weaver claimed that he had engaged in consensual sex with each woman and that each of the women was alive and well when he left them. Their each having died in remarkably similar circumstances on the same night as having met him was just a horrid coincidence that defied imagination.

It certainly did defy imagination. Wheeler-Weaver wanted the jury to believe in the type of coincidence that would be too outlandish to be believed if it appeared in a work of schlock fiction. The jury deliberated for just two hours before returning with unanimous guilty verdicts on three counts of murder, one count of attempted murder, three counts of desecrating a dead body, aggravated arson and aggravated sexual assault. Wheeler-Weaver stood in the courtroom completely impassively as the verdicts were read out.

Due to delays caused by the COVID-19 pandemic, Khalil Wheeler-Weaver wasn't sentenced for his crimes until Wednesday the 6th of October 2021. Before sentence was passed, the surviving victim, Tiffany Taylor, addressed the court, *"My whole life is different,"* Tiffany Taylor said, *"I don't wear makeup anymore; I don't have friends. I'm always paranoid. But I'm happy to still be here... I hope you don't show him any remorse because he's not showing any remorse."*

As he passed sentence, Judge Mark Ali made his feelings clear, *"The purpose of this sentence is that this defendant never walks free in society again,"* Judge Ali said, *"This defendant absolutely lacks remorse."* Judge Ali sentenced Khalil Wheeler-Weaver to 160 years imprisonment, with a minimum of 145 years to be served before he is eligible for parole. Judge Ali concluded, *"The sentence today sends a clear and unequivocal message that each of these young women mattered."*

After receiving his sentence, Wheeler-Weaver remained manipulative and defiant as, despite the strong evidence against him, he continued to deny his guilt. *"The assistant prosecutor, Adam Wells, knowingly and purposefully misled this court and the family of the victims into believing I was the person who committed these crimes."* Wheeler-Weaver said, *"I would like to say that I do feel sympathy for the victims. My heart goes out to their family and friends. However, I was not, and I repeat, I was not the person who committed these crimes. I have clear and convincing evidence that I was set up, lied on, and framed by the Essex County Prosecutors Office."*

It's now suspected that Khalil Wheeler-Weaver had further victims. He is currently awaiting trial for one further murder. On Friday the 7th of October 2016, fifteen-year-old Mawa Doumbia disappeared from her home in Newark. In the weeks leading up to her death, she had been using the app Tagged to talk to a male who had offered her money for sex. The police say that extensive digital investigation indicates that the man Mawa was talking to was Khalil Wheeler-Weaver.

On Sunday the 19th of May 2019, a badly decomposed body was found in an abandoned house in Orange, New Jersey, just a short walk from Khalil Wheeler-Weaver's former home. Tellingly, the victim's head had been wrapped in duct tape, and she had been strangled with a ligature. It wasn't until Friday the 5th of November 2021 that the body was eventually identified as being Mawa's.

On Thursday the 31st of March 2022, Khalil Wheeler-Weaver was charged with Mawa's murder. He is yet to be tried or convicted of this offence in a court of law.

The investigation into Khalil Wheeler-Weaver's crimes stands as a sad testament to how many in society are left behind and treated as second-class citizens because of their race, their mental health conditions and the occupations they have been forced into as a last desperate resort. As Assistant Prosecutor Adams Wells highlighted, it wasn't the police who were the heroes of this case. It was Sarah Butler's sister and friends who were left playing detective. Indeed, if the New Jersey Police had done their job properly and not disregarded Tiffany Taylor because she was a sex worker and a woman of colour, Sarah Butler would still be alive today. The police officers who so monumentally failed in this case faced no disciplinary proceedings and were not sanctioned in any way. It's not surprising, therefore, that the New Jersey Police Department's actions have left some to ask if Khalil Wheeler-Weaver was protected in some way by the New Jersey Police Department due to his familial connections to that police department.

I find it hard and chilling to contemplate that a police department would allow a man to kill and kill again simply because of the family he came from. I have to, therefore, believe it was monumental incompetence and prejudice that allowed Khalil Wheeler-Weaver to get away with murder when he could have been apprehended and incarcerated after killing his first victim. It's a salient lesson for us all to be vigilant to institutional racism and misogyny, to speak out about it, and to never let a man like Khalil Wheel-Weaver get away with such crimes ever again.

Conclusion

Well, there you go. I hope that these cases gave you the frisson of fear and excitement I felt as a child when I first heard about many of them. I don't want you going away feeling too frightened though. In the United Kingdom, the chances of being murdered are infinitesimally small, just 0.00117%, and the chance of being the victim of a random sex killer is even smaller still, just 0.00019%. I'm afraid if you live in the United States, your chances of being a murder victim are a wee bit higher, but nothing to get too concerned about.

Unfortunately, there will always be men who feel it is their right to take what they want by force and violence, but it is a small percentage of the overall population. Better education of young men at an earlier age to teach them that they are not entitled to touch and molest women in any way they want is key to reducing those numbers further. But we are getting there. Most people you will meet are just nice, ordinary people with no sexually violent proclivities whatsoever.

So, until next time, don't have nightmares.

H. N. Lloyd

Bibliography

I hope you have enjoyed reading this volume of the Murder Tales series. If you have then, obviously, please read the other books in the series. Below is a list of other books many of which I found invaluable in the research of this book, and I would encourage you all to read them:

Bloody London – Martin Fido – Apple – 2014

Cause Of Death: Memoirs Of A Home Office Pathologist – Dr Geoffery Garrott and Andrew Nott – Constable & Robinson - 2001

The Dating Game Killer – Jack James – Maplewood Publishing – 2018

More Than Just A Pretty Face – Victoria Best – Amazon - 2020

Rodney James Alcala Occupation: Serial Killer a.k.a The Dating Game Killer – J. R. Murray – Amazon – 2017

Surrey Murders – John Van der Kiste – History Press - 2009

You can purchase other titles in the Murder Tales series here:

UK:
https://www.amazon.co.uk/s?k=Murder+Tales+H.+N.+Lloyd&ref=nb_sb_noss_2

US:
https://www.amazon.com/s?k=Murder+Tales+H.+N.+Lloyd&ref=nb_sb_noss_2

Other titles available in the Murder Tales series:

Murder Tales: Unsolved

Murder Tales: Murder At Christmas

Murder Tales: The Granny Killers

Murder Tales: My Bloody Valentine

Murder Tales: They Got Away With Murder

Murder Tales: The Mummy's Boys

Murder Tales: The Bounders

Murder Tales: The Child Killers

Murder Tales: The JFK Conspiracies

Murder Tales: Till Death Do Us Part

Murder Tales: Jack the Ripper

Murder Tales: Unsolved, Volume II

Murder Tales: Occult Murders

Murder Tales: Child Killers, Volume II

Murder Tales: Ted Bundy

Murder Tales: The Hangman's Tales

Murder Tales: Fatal Fame

Murder Tales: Stranger Than Fiction

Murder Tales: The Poisoners

Murder Tales: Deadly Doctors

End Notes

[i] In many accounts, it categorically states that Whiteway was estranged from his wife. Not a bit of it. The Whiteway's were very much in love, but Mary Jane Elizabeth Whiteway couldn't stand to be around her mother-in-law, Ellen, and the couple couldn't afford their own home. This forced the couple to live apart until they had saved enough money to buy their own home.

[ii] For much more information on all of these fascinating cases, please read 'Murder Tales: The Hangman's Tales.'

[iii] For more information about this terrifying case, please read the warmly received 'Murder Tales: The Yorkshire Ripper.'

[iv] True crime fans may recognise the name, Steve Hodel. He is the author of the barmy but no less entertaining Black Dalia Avenger series of books and their counterpart, Most Evil. In these books, Hodel accuses his father, George Hill Hodel, of not only being the perpetrator of the infamous Black Dalia murder but also accusing him of the infamous Zodiac Killings and being the perpetrator of virtually every other famous unsolved murder in America. For more information on these cases and Steve Hodel's amusing theories, please read 'Murder Tales: Unsolved' and 'Murder Tales: Unsolved Volume II'.

[v] Ellen's mother had an affair with her sister's husband. When the affair was discovered, both couples divorced and Yvonne Hover married her sister's ex-husband, making Ellen and her cousin stepsisters.

[vi] For my many British readers, The Dating Game is the American show that the beloved British game show Blind Date is based on, minus the monstrously egotistical host Cilla Black.

[vii] Browns was known as the Harrods of the North.

[viii] A Honorary Recorder is the chief judge in a given area, this case Mr Justice Clarke was the chief judge for Merseyside.

[ix] bitumen is a black-coloured sticky, viscous liquid derived from petroleum and used in asphalting and damp proofing before the laying of concrete.

[x] Well, law-abiding if you don't count the many incidents of domestic violence against his poor, put-upon wife for which Jackson was never charged or convicted. I'm happy to say that the police no longer turn a blind eye to such horrendous offences, and Jackson no doubt would have had several convictions of a violent nature on his antecedent record if the law had been applied with the zero-tolerance approach that it is today.

[xi] Violet was only sixty-two, so not at all old by today's standards. However, back in 1985, women were classed as Old Age Pensioners when they reached the age of sixty.

[xii] The Auto Garage no longer exists, it was demolished in the early 1990s, and a lumber yard now stands on the site. The entrance to the lumber yard is on Argyle Street South, and the shop front that Diane parked in front of is now replaced by a fence.

[xiii] Parkgate was the name of the road in Darlington where the local Police Station was situated. However, it has been confirmed that no locals ever referred to the Police Station colloquially as

Parkgate.

[xiv] Alex believes he may have been the one to do this; however, being only three at the time his memory of the murder is mercifully fuzzy.

[xv] Stipendiary Magistrates were paid magistrates who acted in the lower courts of the United Kingdom and were referred to when sitting simply as Sir or Ma'am. In the year 2000, the role was replaced by that of District Judges, who are now referred to in court by the title Judge.

[xvi] Despite what you might think, touching silk is not when a barrister has a toilet mishap; it's what those in the legal profession call it when they are appointed to the position of King's Counsel.

[xvii] Michael Stone has been convicted twice of the 1996 murder of mother and daughter Lin and Megan Russell and the attempted murder of Josie Russell. Some of those who worked on the investigation have cast doubt on the guilt of Michael Stone, his conviction hanging entirely upon the jail cell confession of a self-confessed liar. The doubts have been compounded by the confession of serial killer Levi Bellfield, who states he was, in fact, the man who murdered the mother and daughter. Indeed, Bellfield resembles the artist's impression of the man seen by witnesses who was undoubtedly the killer. The Criminal Cases Review Commission refuses to acknowledge the validity of Bellfield's confession, stating that it is *"not credible evidence."*

[xviii] The power to authorise such a release no longer stands with the Home Secretary. This now comes under the purvey of the Secretary of State For Justice, a position created in 2007 when the Home Office was effectively broken into two. This was officially done so that the Home Secretary could focus on matters of policing, homeland security, and terrorism. It was also a politically weakened Tony Blair's attempt to make the Home Secretary role less powerful and significant.

Printed in Great Britain
by Amazon